Secr[illegible] the Sacred Heart

"This work is an easily understood and enthusiastic introduction to the devotion to the Sacred Heart of Jesus as well as one of the devotion's favored practices, the Enthronement of the Sacred Heart in the home."

Rev. David P. Reid, SS.CC.
National Director of the Enthronement Office
Congregation of the Sacred Hearts, United States Province

"Following the structure of the promises of grace given to St. Margaret Mary Alacoque by our Lord, Emily Jaminet outlines a practical, useful, and compelling approach to the devotion to the Sacred Heart. This book serves as a guide not only for all the faithful but also for priests who desire to bring God's people closer to the heart of Jesus."

Rev. Gregory P. Haake, C.S.C.
Assistant Professor of French
University of Notre Dame

"How can we draw our family closer to the Lord and to each other? *Secrets of the Sacred Heart* reveals how a family's devotion to the Sacred Heart of Jesus does both. Highly recommended."

Kimberly Hahn
Coauthor of *Rome Sweet Home*

"On our quest to be like Jesus, we find a fast lane into his heart through a devotion to the Sacred Heart. Emily Jaminet reminds readers of the powerful invitation of healing and heart restoration as well as the promises Jesus has for each of us. Claiming Jesus' promises should be the essential cornerstone in every disciple's home, and this is the book to equip you to claim them."

Megan Schrieber
Coauthor of *Theology of Home*

"Since my family did the enthronement of the Sacred Heart of Jesus, I have been seeking reminders of the powerful promises associated with this devotion. *Secrets of the Sacred Heart* is such a gift! This book is a handy guide for anyone who wants to be inspired for the first time or renewed in their commitment to this life-changing devotion!"

Danielle Bean
Brand manager of CatholicMom.com
Author of *Giving Thanks and Letting Go*

Secrets of the Sacred Heart

TWELVE WAYS TO CLAIM JESUS' PROMISES IN YOUR LIFE

Emily Jaminet
Executive Director
Sacred Heart Enthronement Network

Ave Maria Press AVE Notre Dame, Indiana

Founded in 1865, Ave Maria Press is a ministry of the United States Province of Holy Cross.

www.avemariapress.com

Paperback: ISBN-13 978-1-64680-019-3

E-book: ISBN-13 978-1-64680-020-9

Cover image: *Sacred Heart* © 2020 by Jacqueline Gonzalez, www.etsy.com / shop / ArtbyJackieGonzalez.

Cover and text design by Katherine Robinson.

Printed and bound in the United States of America.

Library of Congress Cataloging-in-Publication Data is available.

TO MY LOVING HUSBAND, JOHN:
YOU ARE MY ROCK.
TO MY PARENTS
WHO INTRODUCED ME
TO THE HEART OF JESUS:
THANK YOU!
AND TO MY CHILDREN,
WHOM I LOVE:
MAY YOUR FAITH IN JESUS
GROW DEEPER EVERY DAY.

Contents

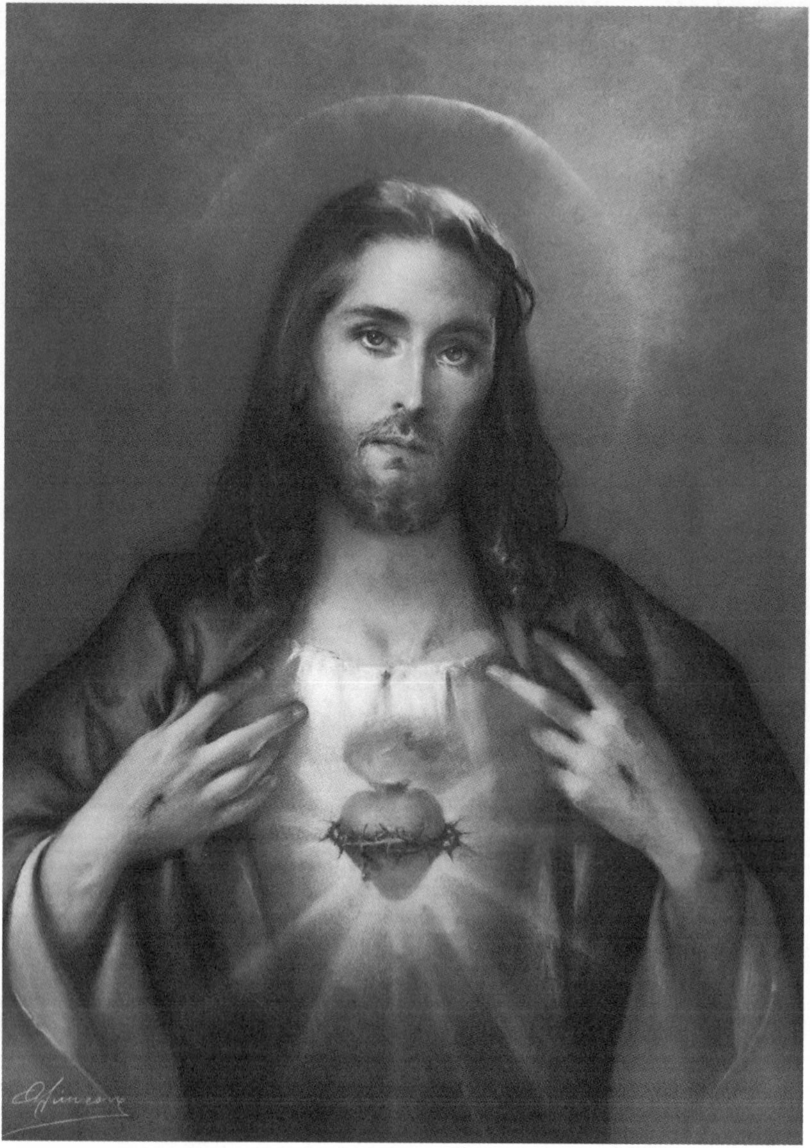

The Twelve Promises of the Sacred Heart of Jesus

1. I will give them all the graces necessary in their state of life.
2. I will establish peace in their homes.
3. I will comfort them in all their afflictions.
4. I will be their secure refuge during life, and above all, in death.
5. I will bestow abundant blessings upon all their undertakings.
6. Sinners will find in my heart the source and infinite ocean of mercy.
7. Lukewarm souls shall become fervent.
8. Fervent souls shall quickly mount to high perfection.
9. I will bless every place in which an image of my Heart is exposed and honored.
10. I will give to priests the gift of touching the most hardened hearts.
11. Those who shall promote this devotion shall have their names written in my Heart.
12. I promise you in the excessive mercy of my Heart that my all-powerful love will grant to all those who receive Holy Communion on the First Fridays in nine consecutive months the grace of final perseverance; they shall not die in my disgrace, nor without receiving their sacraments. My divine Heart shall be their safe refuge in this last moment.

INTRODUCTION

> [Jesus] has loved us all with a human heart. For this reason, the Sacred Heart of Jesus, pierced by our sins and for our salvation, "is quite rightly considered the chief sign and symbol of that . . . love with which the divine Redeemer continually loves the eternal Father and all human beings" without exception.
>
> —*Catechism of the Catholic Church,* 478

When it comes to love, there is no more recognized symbol than the heart. Throughout human history, the human heart has been considered more than an organ, particularly in the areas of philosophy and religion; it represents the place where love lives. The heart "makes us human"; it is our spiritual center and holds great significance.

We read in scripture, "Therefore, you shall love the LORD, your God, with your whole heart, and with your whole being, and with your whole strength. Take to heart these words which I command you today. Keep repeating them to your children. Recite them when you are at home and when you are away, when you lie down and when you get up" (Dt 6:5–7). It is no wonder, then, that the Lord invites us to come to know him and to love him through a powerful devotion to his heart. The

Sacred Heart devotion leads us closer to authentic love as Christ infuses our wounded hearts with his divine life, in a kind of mystical "heart transplant."

This is a message very dear to me, for I have experienced the power of the Sacred Heart devotion in the life of my family. We have received extraordinary graces and supernatural help through practicing the Sacred Heart devotion. I have personally witnessed now three generations of family members committed to this devotion and experienced firsthand its transformative power. Instead of turning to the pleasures of this world, so broken from sin, we have experienced true fulfillment through the great and wonderful heart of Jesus.

Yes, love comes into our lives through his heart. The Lord wants us to pass this love on to others, from one generation to the next. You cannot love without engaging the heart; the heart is the place where love grows, where love is strengthened and spread to others. It is fitting that we think of the heart in this way, as the heart resides at our core and pumps blood throughout our bodies, out to our extremities in order that we may live. So too does love emanate from our core, sustaining our souls and radiating outward to others. Love is meant to be pumped not only into our actions but also into our interactions and relationships with family, friends, and all those who cross our paths.

A DEVOTION FOR OUR TIME

Our world is in desperate need of Christ's perfect love and would benefit greatly from reconnecting with the "heartbeat" of God. We need to fill ourselves with the love of Christ and allow his authentic, perfect love to renew us, transform us, and purify our understanding of what it is to love through a deep and personal relationship with his Sacred Heart. Without Jesus, we are truly lost and hopeless, for we were created with an inner longing to connect with our Creator. Until that happens, we will continue to search until we discover real and lasting love rooted in the heart of Christ. This love heals our deepest wounds and provides for our deepest needs.

As adopted sons and daughters of God, the Father loves us with an unfathomable love. The devotion to the Sacred Heart, then, is a sort of spiritual roadmap, given to us by Christ to help us find our way home to the heart of the Trinity, the source of all love. The further we go along the route, the closer we draw to that heart, the more it enlivens us, the more we are able to radiate it out to others, and the more fully alive we become!

Although this devotion to the Sacred Heart traces back to the beginning of the Church, it is perhaps more relevant now than it ever was. The Sacred Heart devotion is for all of us, right where we are, now. In a world that continues to grow colder and more confused, Jesus' Sacred Heart sets our hearts on fire with his love in order to burn off the bondages of sin.

Jesus desires us not only to know his heart but also to utterly abandon ourselves to that divine love, to experience it through the rich traditions and powerful teaching and worship that point to the love of our Savior. Now, more than ever before, we need Christ's authentic love to penetrate our hearts and homes and shine forth to others—beginning in our own homes and radiating out into the whole world. This devotion has the potential to transform individuals, homes, communities, workplaces, schools, and every corner of our society. We know this without a doubt, for Christ has sent many holy messengers throughout the history of the Church to deliver his message. In the appendix, you will find a brief history of this devotion in the life of the Catholic Church and more about its primary heralds, but none was more influential in bringing this devotion to fruition than St. Margaret Mary Alacoque.

THE PROMISES OF THE SACRED HEART

Our Lord Jesus Christ appeared to St. Margaret Mary in a series of visions that occurred between 1673 and 1675. During that time, she heard Jesus make several promises to those who would respond to the pleading of his heart and make an effort to return his love. These promises will provide the structure of this book, with a chapter devoted to each.

Within each chapter, you will be introduced to the promise, examine its meaning, ponder its impact in your life, pray about it, and consider what action you can take to practice it in your daily life. You might consider offering the prayer of the Litany of the Sacred Heart (see appendix 2) at the end of each chapter to grow closer to the heart of Jesus. While this book can certainly be read as you would any book, the format of this book is especially well suited for use on a self-paced individual retreat or in a group book study.

The twelve promises, which are listed on page ix of this book facing the traditional Image of the Sacred Heart of Jesus, are the lifeblood of the Sacred Heart devotion. Ever since the Lord shared these promises with St. Margaret Mary, this devotion has become a lifeline of help for believers for hundreds of years. This is evident in the trail of writings and letters associated with this devotion written by popes and saints:

- In 1765, Pope Clement XIII approved the Feast of the Sacred Heart for the bishops of Poland and the Roman Archconfraternity of the Sacred Heart.
- In 1856, Pope Pius IX extended the feast to the universal Church.
- In 1899, Pope Leo XIII wrote the encyclical letter *Annum Sacrum*, saying, "In that Sacred Heart all our hopes should be placed, and from it the salvation of men is to be confidently sought" (*AS*, 12). On June 11 of that same year, the Holy Father consecrated the human race to the Sacred Heart of Jesus, calling this one act "the greatest act of my pontificate."[1]
- In 1928, Pope Pius XI wrote *Miserentissimus Redemptor* on the reparation due to the Sacred Heart.
- In 1956, Pius XII wrote *Haurietis Aquas* on the nature of the true devotion to the heart of Jesus.

St. John Paul II and all popes since have held this devotion in high esteem as well. This devotion is sincere and offers many avenues by which to grow in your faith, all of which we will examine in the following chapters. It is a secure means by which to help you grow in your love for Christ.

ARE THESE PROMISES BASED IN SCRIPTURE?

The promises of the Sacred Heart serve as reminders of the essential aspects of this devotion, but even more, they are rooted in the covenant promises of scripture. In the Old Testament, going all the way back to Abraham, God entered into a covenant first with Abram (see Genesis 15), then later with Moses (see Exodus 19–34), and then with Joshua, promising that Joshua would lead the Chosen People into the Promised Land (see Joshua 1). Even when the Israelites lost their way and worshipped the golden calf, God did not rescind his promise, for our God is trustworthy.

In the New Testament, we find these covenants fulfilled when God sends his only Son, Jesus, "the way and the truth and the life" (Jn 14:6), to help us on our journey in search of eternal life. The promises of the Sacred Heart are similar to the Beatitudes (see Matthew 5:3–12), in that they are both like stepping stones on a path leading us to Jesus. By following them, we draw nearer to Christ and experience the natural consequence of blessings from our Lord, who is ever faithful. Because he is faithful, we put our trust in his promises and believe we will ultimately experience life with him in eternity.

In his work *Understanding the Heart,* Fr. Francis Larkin, SS.CC., writes, "What is new in these promises is therefore not their content, but the circumstances of their fulfillment, in fact what has already been promised in substance in the Gospels, is now attached precisely to devotion to the Sacred Heart."[2] Popes have written about it, saints have lived it, and generations of Catholics have shown us the impact it can have on our lives. Ordinary people have experienced extraordinary grace in their lives, and so can you.

Jesus is always the Seeker. He knocks upon our hearts, searching, seeking, and longing for us to develop a personal relationship with him. "For the Son of Man has come to seek and to save what was lost." (Lk 19:10). Our Lord wants a relationship with us, but the question is, do we want one with him? Jesus brings us close to his heart and desires that we grow in holiness and help others encounter his heart. Jesus wants to transform us through his heart, which is a fiery furnace of love. This devotion offers us the heart transplant we desire and stability in an unstable world. Jesus calls us to place our trust in his heart and allow him to transform us. May this book be an instrument of that transformation by fostering in you a devotion to the Sacred Heart of Jesus!

1

Allow Grace to Fill Your Life

Promise #1

I will give them all the graces necessary in their state of life.

Our Lord will grant you many graces if you have the courage to follow him.

—St. Margaret Mary[1]

One day my mom came over with a special gift for me: she had just found a beautiful set of holy images, more than a hundred years old, from a local antique mall. They still hang in my front room: the Sacred Heart of Jesus and Immaculate Heart of Mary.

That first night she gave them to me, I felt a great desire to kneel down and pray beneath the beautiful image of the Sacred Heart of Jesus. As I gazed upon the image, the flames rising from his heart seemed brighter than the sun. The crown of thorns that surrounded it was a painful reminder of the grief and suffering inflicted upon him by our sins; the cross embedded at the top of the heart spoke eloquently of his death, a death that was necessary to bring me close to the Father. And like every Sacred Heart image, this one had a tiny piercing, reminding me of the blood and water that flowed out into the world, washing and cleansing all those who draw near.

I can still recall that moment: kneeling before my Sacred Heart image and saying to Jesus, "I am yours, and you need to help me." I knew I didn't need to wait until I was in a church to pray; Jesus was right there in my very home, my own domestic church, and so I laid my greatest concern at the time at his feet and asked for help.

At that time I was feeling a particularly strong need for spiritual guidance and direction. While the early years of homeschooling had been fruitful and happy, as my children aged, and as more kids were thrown in the mix and the breadth and depth of the subject matter increased, I was becoming increasingly aware of gaps I knew I couldn't fill on my own. Even so, I found it extremely difficult to let go of what I thought was the only way to fulfill my responsibility. I knew we needed to make a change, but I was uncertain how to take the next step forward.

Praying to the Sacred Heart—both on my own and with my husband—provided tremendous graces and imparted a sense of clarity we hadn't experienced before. It helped us work through our concerns and resulted in a decision to put all the kids in Catholic school. We also decided to move to a new home, closer to the school, in order to reduce travel time in the car and allow us to be part of the local church community. While taking the first step was difficult, through it all we felt the Lord was leading us, and we continue to marvel at the many blessings we have received as a result of giving our lives over to the Sacred Heart.

EXPLORING THE PROMISE

I will give them all the graces necessary in their state of life. Often when we refer to one's "state of life," we think in terms of one's vocation as an ordained religious, a married person, or a single layperson. However, our state of life doesn't end there. In life, we don't just need graces to decide whom we are to marry or how we are going to serve the Lord; we also need graces to live out our vocation each and every day.

In the book of Ecclesiastes, we find that "God has made everything appropriate to its time" (Eccl 3:11). Our state of life is always changing, even if our vocation stays the same. Just as the seasons of nature turn and change, the cycle of life continues on. Jesus wants to offer us his graces and eternal perspective on where we are and what is affecting us now. Regardless of your age or situation, and wherever you are on your faith journey, Christ still wants to walk with you and offer you his graces each moment. "I am the way and the truth and the life," the Lord tells us. "No one comes to the Father except through me." (Jn 14:6). Jesus is offering us a path to experience the Father; this path is the road that leads to our eternal home.

The *Catechism* tells us that "grace is a *participation in the life of God*" (CCC, 1997). Through our baptism, we are introduced as adopted children into intimate union not just with Jesus but also with the life of the Trinity as we participate in the life of the Church, the Body of Christ here on earth.

Jesus is offering us grace today! He wants to help us in our weakness to overcome our difficulties. So often we limit God and fill our minds with negative statements such as "I can't do that" instead of saying, "I have the strength for everything through him who empowers me" (Phil 4:13). We are called to change our mindset and seek new graces to strengthen us in our weakness.

Think of St. Paul, whose unbridled zeal once made him a persecutor of the Church, and whose unnamed "thorn of the flesh" (see 2 Corinthians 12:7) caused him such suffering. The Lord did not remove this weakness, despite Paul's urgent pleas; rather, the Lord assured the apostle, "My grace is sufficient for you, for power is made perfect in weakness." Paul continues, "I will rather boast most gladly of my weaknesses, in order that the power of Christ may dwell with me. Therefore, I am content with weaknesses, insults, hardships, persecutions, and constraints, for the sake of Christ; for when I am weak, then I am strong" (2 Cor 12:9–10).

In practicing a devotion to the Sacred Heart, we are constantly seeking new graces through discovering Jesus' holy heart, the fount of all love. When we struggle, we need to seek out these graces so we can better see him, love him, and experience the strength he is offering. All we have to do is remember that Jesus is offering us graces for our state in life—here, today—and respond.

PONDERING THE PROMISE

It is easy to be so busy or consumed by the worries of the day that you forget to bring them to prayer. Shut your eyes and ask Jesus to show you how much he loves you and to point out an area in your life that could benefit from an infusion of his strength. Then take a few moments to reflect on the following:

1. Do you seek a personal relationship with the Lord and allow him to help you with your daily trials, whether in serious matters or trivial moments? How does faith play out in your life?
2. Think about your state in life. In what areas do you need more grace? Are you struggling with an aspect of your life that you need to surrender to the Lord? Do you have pain or hurt that needs to be tossed into his great furnace of love?
3. Think about how you can take steps to grow in faith and welcome Jesus into your heart. Do you believe that at the end of time, "the Kingdom of God will come in its fullness" and "the just will reign with Christ forever" (*CCC*, 1060; 1 Cor 15:28)? How does this impact the way you live your life today?

PRAYING THE PROMISE

Perhaps the best first step toward growing in our relationship with Christ is to place our trust in him by offering ourselves up to his care. In her autobiography, St. Margaret Mary shares, "He wishes the consecration of individuals, families, and nations to his Heart."[2] Pope Leo XIII explained, "For by consecrating ourselves to him we not only declare our open and free acknowledgement and acceptance of his authority over us, but we also testify that if what we offer as a gift were really our own, we would still offer it with our whole heart."[3]

Have you consecrated yourself to the Sacred Heart of Jesus? If not—or if you would like to renew your intention, either now or after a First Friday Mass (see chapter 12)—consider reciting this special prayer of consecration written by St. Margaret Mary.[4]

Consecration to the Sacred Heart of Jesus

O Sacred Heart of my Lord and Savior Jesus Christ, to Thee I consecrate and offer up my person and my life, my actions, trials, and sufferings, that my entire being may henceforth only be employed in loving, honoring and glorifying Thee. This is my irrevocable will, to belong entirely to Thee, and to do all for Thy love, renouncing with my whole heart all that can displease Thee.

I take Thee, O Sacred Heart, for the sole object of my love, the protection of my life, the pledge of my salvation, the remedy of my frailty and inconstancy, the reparation for all the defects of my life, and my secure refuge at the hour of my death. Be Thou, O Most Merciful Heart, my justification before God Thy Father, and screen me from his anger which I have so justly merited. I fear all from my own weakness and malice, but placing my entire confidence in Thee, O Heart of Love, I hope all from Thine infinite Goodness. Annihilate in me all that can displease or resist Thee. Imprint Thy pure love so deeply in my heart that I may never forget Thee or be separated from Thee.

I beseech Thee, through Thine infinite Goodness, grant that my name be engraved upon Thy Heart, for in this I place all my happiness and all my glory, to live and to die as one of Thy devoted servants.

Amen.

PRACTICING THE PROMISE

After praying this powerful prayer of the Sacred Heart, reflect on what it means to welcome Jesus. Go to welcomehisheart.com, and watch the free video *To Whom Do You Belong*, by Fr. Stash Dailey.

Ask Jesus to show you what areas of your life you should surrender to him. What parts of your heart need healing? This healing could be spiritual, physical, emotional, or psychological.

Reflect on what your life would look like if you allowed Jesus into your heart and home. If time permits, I recommend taking a few minutes to pray the Litany of the Sacred Heart of Jesus at the end of this book in appendix 2 .

2

WELCOME CHRIST'S PEACE IN YOUR HOME

Promise #2

I will establish peace in their homes.

> Establish your dwelling in the amiable Heart of Jesus, and you will find unalterable peace, strength to carry out all your good desires, and protection against voluntary faults.
>
> —St. Margaret Mary[1]

An "enthronement" is a special act of consecration done by a family or individual who wishes to welcome Jesus into their home (or other dedication space such as a school or place of business) as King, Savior, Brother, and Friend. The ceremony includes special prayers as well as placing (or "enthroning") an image of the Sacred Heart of Jesus in a place of importance. The intention of an enthronement is to signify the intention of all those present to grow closer to God and to allow him to enlighten their souls with Divine Truth.

Perhaps the most gratifying part of my work directing a ministry that promotes enthronement to the Sacred Heart is that I constantly receive testimonies from individuals and families whose lives have been touched in amazing ways by this devotion. Very often, it is this the second promise in particular that attracted them to the devotion.

This should come as no surprise. Ultimately, we all want peace in life—a sense that all is right in our world, the absence of conflict or worry, and a feeling of contentment and even joy. We long for the greatest Gospel promise available, the peace of the Lord. "Peace I leave with you . . . my peace I give to you" (Jn 14:27). For many who practice the Sacred Heart devotion, this type of peace is exactly what they frequently experience.

One married couple recently shared with me that, after they enthroned the Sacred Heart in their home, they experienced a restoration of not only faith but also peace, peace where there was once yelling, arguing, and a restlessness that kept the family distant and distracted from knowing the value of who they were and the treasure they had in each other.

"After the enthronement to the Sacred Heart, I didn't want to turn to television as my source of comfort and a place to escape," the wife said. "Rather, I began to enjoy the silence, the new peace that filled my house not from the noise and distraction of screens but from knowing Jesus was here. My husband and I started to connect and share on a new level, and we found a peace in knowing that the Lord wanted to walk this journey with us."

Another family shared that after the enthronement, both the parents stopped drinking and the culture of the family changed. The father writes,

> We became a more peaceful family; when we eliminated the destructive behaviors that were hurting our family, we began to place our total focus on our children and our marriage. We were able to forgive each other for the past hurts from the drinking, partying, and worldly delights that were distracting me from my real mission to be holy and share my faith with my family and others. I now want to be the best spouse and father to my children. The enthronement to the Sacred Heart, offered hope to our family and a peace that was beyond any understanding because, as we read from St. Augustine, "I am restless until I rest in you."

A teenager observed that when there is peace in the home that is rooted in faith and when the devotion to the Sacred Heart is alive, there is a basic code of Christian respect. Each person seeks to serve and seeks to love. Parents don't go out of their way to stir up restlessness in each other. Removing anger is a great way to restore peace.

So often that peace must begin inside the hearts of the parents. As one father shared,

> I have discovered that the grace of peace begins with me, in desiring to be a peacemaker. I came to realize that I really want a relationship with my

> family members, and not being prideful is a great way to begin. I now say I am sorry when I have hurt them and seek peace when I can. I have come to appreciate peacemakers and those who long to spread God's peace to others; my desire is that I can pass that on to my children and hopefully to their children.

Of course, no family is perfect. We all have things that rob us of peace. Yet through all our struggles, we can be comforted by the knowledge that Christ is there for us and offers us his peace if we place our trust in the Lord. St. Margaret Mary reminds us, "May the peace of the adorable Heart of Jesus Christ ever fill our hearts, so that nothing may be able to disturb our serenity" (II, 263).[2] I believe that whether it is through personal experience or through the testimony of others, cultivating a devotion to the Sacred Heart is inviting Jesus—the King of peace, love, and mercy—into your heart and home.

EXPLORING THE PROMISE

Peace is one of the heavenly gifts we seek most, yet rarely do we know how to find it. Peace is not tangible, but you can sure tell when it is not there, especially in our restless hearts. The *Catechism* teaches us that peace is "the tranquility of order. Peace is the work of justice and the effect of charity" (CCC, 2304). And yet it is not simply a human effort, for "earthly peace is the image and fruit of the peace of Christ, the messianic Prince of Peace" (CCC, 2305).

St. Teresa of Calcutta often said, "If you want to change the world, go home and love your family." It is possessing not the wealth of the world but a true longing for love in our hearts and homes that bears the fruit of peace. When we lack peace in our hearts, we are restless and anxious about the world and the problems that fill it. St. Augustine reminds us, "Our hearts are restless until they rest in the Lord."[3]

When we lack peace, it prevents us from seeing God's hand, especially in times of struggle and difficulty. Often, fear and anxiety steal our peace and we begin to tremble and worry. Jesus wants to exchange our restless, broken hearts for his heart that is full of peace. Jesus wants us to experience this peace despite whatever trials we are suffering. He wants us to have hope that peace is even possible. Listen again to his words of comfort: "Peace I leave with you; my peace I give to you. Not as the world gives do I give it to you. Do not let your hearts be troubled or afraid" (Jn 14:27).

Our modern society tempts us to believe that the cure for a restless spirit and conflict within our souls is materialism, pleasure, wealth, and power. Families are under tremendous stress, which affects the basic foundation of our society. As I am writing this book, the whole country—the whole world—is coping with the effects of COVID-19, which has greatly affected our collective sense of well-being. For many of us, it has been a powerful reminder of what happens if we do not seek the peace of the Lord; we can lose our spiritual footing and spiral into depression and anxiety.

The Sacred Heart devotion provides hope, healing, and peace to families needing to be restored and made whole again. It is also a source of powerful graces for all of us seeking to grow in holiness; this devotion will help you to usher these graces into your home and to grow in faith. Are you willing to do that?

No doubt you will almost immediately think of reasons to set aside this invitation. Remember that Satan is always poised for attack, trying to steal our peace. St. Margaret Mary tells us, "Bury all your misery in the mercy of the loving Heart of Jesus and think of nothing but of pleasing him. . . . Henceforth let him do all that He wills in you, with you and for you."[4]

Are you ready to welcome Jesus into the heart of your family? He is knocking at the door to your heart and home. He wants to dine with you; he wants to be part of the culture of your family—just as he sought to be part of the family life of his friends Mary, and Martha, and Lazarus at Bethany.

The scriptures tell us a great deal about these friends of Jesus, whose home was less than three miles away from Jerusalem. Mary, Martha, and Lazarus offered him rest and friendship during his earthly journey, and their home was the backdrop for many powerful teaching moments by our Lord. This was where Jesus brought Lazarus back to life, instructed Mary and Martha on what it means to follow him, and started his great walk to Jerusalem on Palm Sunday.

These three siblings welcomed Jesus into their life, and for it they were forever blessed. We too will receive blessings if we draw close to Christ and allow him to show us the way. Often we allow ourselves to be distracted by our busy lives, forget what truly matters, and lose our peace. When we bring our concerns to Christ, we make ourselves available to his gentle counsel that helps to refocus us. "Martha, burdened with much serving, came to him and said, 'Lord, do you not care that my sister has left me by myself to do the serving? Tell her to help me.' The Lord said to her in reply, "Martha, Martha, you are anxious and worried about many things. . . . Mary has chosen the better part and it will not be taken from her" (Lk 10:40–42).

One version of the enthronement ceremony, credited to Fr. Mateo Crawley-Boevey, reads, "Help make this home another Bethany, where you will always find yourself among friends."[5] This powerful line points to a family of believers who welcomed Jesus and invited him into their life. They shared their hurts, their pains, and their conflict and sought his advice. We too can develop a relationship with the Lord as did Mary, Martha, and Lazarus and create a culture within our walls that allows peace to blossom.

PONDERING THE PROMISE

Take a few minutes and allow your mind to ponder this powerful promise that revolves around the great gift of the Lord's peace. In life, it is easy to be so busy or consumed by the worries of the day that you forget to bring them to prayer. Shut your eyes, and ask Jesus to show you how much he loves you and an area in your life that you need his strength. Then take a moment to consider the following:

1. "My peace I give to you." Do you believe that the Lord is offering you his peace? Do you believe that

your heart and home can be transformed through new graces?

2. What is burdening your heart? In what area do you need transformation? What burdens you and prevents you from forgiving? Does your hard heart block you from experiencing his Sacred Heart?
3. "Mary has chosen the better part and it will not be taken from her" (Lk 10:42). Do we seek to allow others to take our peace? Do we stir up restlessness in others? Could we seek to follow the ways of Jesus and learn how to break bad habits that steal the peace in our hearts and homes? What habits need to change?

PRAYING THE PROMISE

One of the greatest examples of a peacemaker is St. Francis of Assisi, whom Jesus gave to Margaret Mary as a special spiritual guide.[6] St. Francis not only learned what it meant to love Christ and grow in holiness but also greatly affected the entire Catholic Church through the renewal that began in his little *yes* when the Lord asked Francis to "rebuild my church." This is what we need now, a rebuilding of the Church, with the Sacred Heart as the focus. For love brings peace, and peace brings transformation that radiates not only to our own soul but outward to others as well. So take a few minutes to slowly pray this prayer popularly attributed to St. Francis, and reflect on what it means to be an instrument of peace.

PRAYER OF ST. FRANCIS OF ASSISI

Lord, make me an instrument of your peace.
Where there is hatred let me sow love;
Where there is injury, pardon;
Where there is doubt, faith;
Where there is despair, hope;
Where there is darkness, light;
Where there is sadness, joy.

O Divine Master, grant that I may not so much seek
To be consoled as to console;
To be understood as to understand;
To be loved as to love.
For it is in giving that we receive;
It is in pardoning that we are pardoned;
And it is in dying that we are born to eternal life.
Amen.[7]

PRACTICING THE PROMISE

One powerful way to welcome Christ's peace in your home is to pray "small prayers of aspiration" when you pass your image of the Sacred Heart of Jesus. This is a great way to start to notice our Lord in the midst of your daily life and the life of your family.

These little prayers come from the heart, almost in union with each breath.

> Jesus, I trust in you.
> Jesus, I love you.
> Make my home in your heart.

These brief aspirations are so spontaneous and simple, and yet they have the power to transform your life. Just tell Jesus, in your own words, what you are feeling each time you pass in front of his image. Say what you feel called to say before his holy heart. Once you begin this practice, you may find yourself turning to Jesus more and more often in your daily thoughts. This in turn will help you to build up a healthy response to stress and anxiety. Just turn your worries over to the heart of Jesus, and let him fill you with his peace.

The final step in establishing peace in your home involves becoming an instrument of peace yourself. This begins by forgiving all who have hurt you. Jesus urges us to pray, "Forgive us our debts, as we forgive our debtors" (Mt 6:12). May nothing hold you captive and prevent you from offering peace to your family and those around you.

As we close this chapter, please turn to appendix 2 and offer the Litany of the Sacred Heart of Jesus.

3

OFFER YOUR STRUGGLES TO JESUS

Promise #3

I will comfort them in all their afflictions.

It is altogether impossible to enumerate the heavenly gifts which devotion to the Sacred Heart of Jesus has poured out on the souls of the faithful, purifying them, offering them heavenly strength, rousing them to attainment of all virtues.

—Venerable Pope Pius XII[1]

A few years ago, I met a woman who had a deep devotion to the Sacred Heart of Jesus. Each day she turned on a little battery-operated candle under her images of the Sacred Heart of Jesus and Immaculate Heart of Mary, and prayed before them. She had been married two times, each time she married someone who left her abused, battered, and broken. After her second marriage, she realized, "I don't need to find a man to be happy; I have Jesus."

So she turned to the Sacred Heart of Jesus and the Immaculate Heart of Mary, and began praying for her previous spouses and that the hurtful behaviors of her past were not passed to her children or grandchildren. She told me, "I sure don't know how to 'pick them,' so I am best living the rest of my years single for the Lord and caring for my children and grandchildren." This powerful story is a tremendous example of how this devotion can give us a completely new perspective on our lives and daily trials. Jesus wants to lead all of us by the hand when we are suffering and need comfort.

As a wife and mother, I too see the need to hand the Lord my areas of hurt. So often we can forget that Jesus is offering us his heart as a sign of his love for us. We too need to keep loving despite the pain and hurts that take place in the family. As I have needed to forgive my husband, children, and others, they too need to forgive me for my sinful ways.

EXPLORING THE PROMISE

All afflictions in life, great or small, are best understood in relation to the Holy Cross. Jesus suffered not only physically by dying on the Cross but emotionally as well. He sweat blood from the stress and agony of knowing how much he would suffer, and his heart was broken by the betrayal of his closest friends. "My soul is sorrowful even to death. Remain here and keep watch with me" (Mt 26:38).

The most Sacred Heart of Jesus, who was true God and true Man, was broken so that we could be saved. "Insult has broken my heart, and I despair; I looked for compassion, but there was none, for comforters, but found none" (Ps 69:21). He was broken so we could turn to him when we are plagued and need true comfort. The world cannot offer what Christ offers: true compassion and the graces we need to endure.

St. Margaret Mary understood this: "Jesus never promised He would remove all crosses and trials, but rather that He would give us special graces to bear them."[2] Jesus was her only source of comfort, and she was very aware that his heart was the solution to all suffering. "Crosses, contempt, sorrows and afflictions are the real treasures of the lovers of Jesus Christ crucified."[3] For it is only through the crucifixion that we can understand true suffering. For Christians, the crucifix is where we elicit strength to endure our struggles and difficulties and where we find hope.

We learn in scripture that grace is greater than sin. "The law entered in so that transgression might increase but, where sin increased, grace overflowed all the more, so that, as sin reigned in death, grace also might reign through justification for eternal life through Jesus Christ our Lord" (Rom 5:20–21). The Lord is offering us strength when we are weak, comfort when we are broken, and consolation when life seems unbearable. Grace is the solution to how we are to navigate our trials and tribulations and gain the new state of the mind to take each step forward.

The key to gaining grace and dealing with our afflictions is understanding the value of our suffering. St. Margaret Mary shares with us, "He who loves thinks he suffers nothing, even under most cruel torments, and you admit that one cannot love without suffering and that the love of God is a pitiless tyrant which never says it is enough! But it is good to live and die under its tyranny."[4] This powerful quote points to the great mystery of the power of love.

When we choose to connect love with suffering, we are able to love like Christ. Our King stands in opposition to the tyrants of this world, who cause others to suffer for their gain. Instead, he is the one who suffers for us for our benefit. Jesus never says, "enough is enough," "my love has limits," or "I will love you if . . ." His love never ends. Jesus proved this by stretching himself out on the Cross and dying for us, and we know that he would do this over and over again, to save souls.

It is the powerful realization of how much God loves us that enables us to believe the promise of comfort from our daily afflictions. Love changes everything, love is the power that transforms lives; it renews us and helps us to turn outward. "This is my commandment: love one another as I love you. . . . I have called you friends, because I have told you everything I have heard from my Father. It was not you who chose me, but I who chose you and appointed you to go and bear fruit that will remain, so that whatever you ask the Father in my name he may give you. This I command you: love one another" (Jn 15:12, 15–17).

Jesus offers his love to us freely and knows that this love will transform our lives and has the ability to transform others through us. Make no mistake, this transforming love is not something we summon up ourselves; all real love comes from God the Father. We are merely instruments of this love, passing his love to others. Love of Christ is the central aspect of the Sacred Heart devotion.

"Blessed be the God and Father of our Lord Jesus Christ, the Father of compassion and God of all encouragement, who encourages us in our every affliction, so that we may be able to encourage those who are in any affliction with the encouragement with which we ourselves are encouraged by God" (2 Cor 1:3–4).

PONDERING THE PROMISE

Jesus is always offering us his heart, and he desires that we come to know him as the great King of love. Take a few minutes and allow your mind to absorb this powerful promise of comfort the Lord is offering. Then take a few moments to ponder the following:

1. Do you believe that the Lord is offering you his comfort? As a family, do you seek comfort from God in troubled times—or are you more likely to "tune out" with temporary distractions?
2. What are your typical coping skills when it comes to suffering? Do you run from suffering? Do you complain about it? Do you choose worldly pleasures to distract you from it?

3. "This is my commandment: love one another as I love you. No one has greater love than this, to lay down one's life for one's friends" (Jn 15:12–13). Do you know God loves you? How does this understanding help you in affliction?

PRAYING THE PROMISE

One of the great prayers related to the Sacred Heart is the Daily Offering (sometimes called a Morning Offering). I remember walking into my grandparents' bathroom and seeing a sticker of this prayer with a picture of Jesus and his Sacred Heart on the mirror, reminding them to pray to the Sacred Heart each morning. I now keep the same prayer on my mirror along with the final words from St. Francis Assisi: "My brothers, we must begin to serve our Lord and God. Until now we have done very little."[5]

The Daily Offering is a wonderful way to gain more grace and offer your day to the Sacred Heart of Jesus. This simple prayer allows us to turn our daily afflictions into gifts of love back to his most Sacred Heart.

The following prayer is believed to have been written by Fr. Francois Xavier Gautrelet, S.J., the founder of the Apostleship of Prayer. Founded in 1844 in Vals, France, this apostleship is an association whose members "seek not only their own salvation but through prayer and sacrifice seek the growth of the Mystical Body of Christ and the spread of his Kingdom upon earth."[6] The individuals that pray this Morning Offering wrap all their "prayers, works, joys and sufferings" into the heart of Jesus.

THE MORNING OFFERING

O Jesus, through the Immaculate Heart of Mary, I offer you my prayers, works, joys and sufferings of this day in union with the Holy Sacrifice of the Mass throughout the world. I offer them for all the intentions of your Sacred Heart: for the salvation of souls, for reparations for sin, and for the reunion of all Christians. I make this offering for the intentions of our bishops and of all Apostles of Prayer, and in particular for those intentions recommended by our Holy Father this month.

Amen.

PRACTICING THE PROMISE

Start your day in prayer. Wake up a few minutes earlier than you typically do, and seek his graces by reciting the prayer above. Post this prayer in a place where you will see it first thing in the morning. (I have mine posted on my bathroom mirror so I'll see it when I brush my teeth.) As you go about your day, make a conscious effort to identify your struggles, mentally bundle them up, and offer them to Christ.

Lastly, consider doing acts of reparation during your day. One of the most significant aspects of this devotion is that we can "offer up our joys and sufferings" on behalf of others. These acts of reparation can be as simple as not putting sugar in your coffee to eating only bread and water throughout a day of fasting.

Jesus wants us to detach from this world; making acts of reparation can be a great help! I remember as a young mom I found that motherhood provided many opportunities to offer up my trials, such as lack of sleep or extra cooking and cleaning! What can you give back to the Lord?

In closing, please take a moment to offer the Litany of the Sacred Heart of Jesus (in appendix 2.).

4

Take Refuge in Jesus

Promise #4

I will be their secure refuge during life, and above all, in death.

> This divine and loving Heart is my hope and my refuge; its merits are my salvation, my life and my resurrection.
>
> —St. Margaret Mary[1]

In life or in death, we need to learn how to turn to Jesus as our safe haven. I have witnessed firsthand how this promise has been fulfilled in the life of my relatives on my mother's side. I tell people that I am "fourth-generation Sacred Heart," because of the spiritual legacy of my family, which goes back at least that far.

For my mother's parents and my great-aunts and great-uncles, devotion to the Sacred Heart was a way of life; they attempted to do everything—and encouraged those around them to act—in a manner pleasing to God. We call them "the Greats" since they were virtuous and exceptional in the midst of their ordinary lives. They didn't have excess wealth, they worked really hard in ordinary jobs, and yet they lived a life without any wants and with so much joy! These Greats taught me not only how to live a life ablaze with the love of God but also how to die in the state of grace by trusting in the heart of Jesus.

One relative that had a particularly strong influence on me was my great-uncle Bud. He was a gentle, faithful, virtuous man who lived a life of service to his family and others. His warmth and easy manner made all feel welcome and genuinely loved. In short, he exemplified everything one would hope to become by the end of one's life on earth. One day, during a conversation with my mom, he shared a beautiful prayer that he would recite daily, to which he attributed many graces. This prayer had given him strength for the journey and allowed him to trust in the Lord. My mom nicknamed it "Bud's prayer," but we later discovered that it goes by another title, "A Prayer for Myself." She asked him for a copy of the prayer, so she could share it with others.

The day after my mother's encounter with Great-Uncle Bud, we received the sad news that he had passed away in his apartment from an apparent heart attack. Later, when my parent went to his apartment to help deal with his effects, my mother noticed something on the kitchen counter. My great-uncle Bud had placed this very prayer, which was on the back of a prayer card, in an envelope to mail to my mother to fulfill his promise to share this powerful prayer. Since that night, my parents along with other organizations in my hometown have distributed more than twenty thousand of these prayer cards throughout our local community and beyond.

You will have an opportunity to offer this traditional Sacred Heart devotional prayer yourself a bit later in this chapter, in the section "Praying the Promise."

EXPLORING THE PROMISE

Recently, I was at a Sacred Heart prayer gathering where, at the end of the night, we prayed for all the intentions we held in our heart. As we went around the room, each person shared a pressing need seemingly more urgent than the one before, and yet the whole experience was so very beautiful and faith-filled. As each local promoter of the Sacred Heart shared their personal prayer intentions, they trusted that the Lord would be their refuge in this life and in the moment of death. They knew that what they and the families they served needed was more grace and love.

On nights like these, I am reminded that we are called to bring the people and situations that we carry in our hearts to prayer. The troubles of life can cause us to be overwhelmed, and yet God has a better plan for us to bring these intentions to his holy heart so he can act and provide us with the strength we need.

When life tosses us lemons, do we make lemonade? Without sugar, the sourness of the lemon is overpowering. The love of God is like sugar that transforms our hearts so that our sufferings in life have a kind of sweetness, meaning, and purpose. God's love renews: it inspires, it restores, it transforms, and it strengthens our endurance. This love, poured out of his most Sacred Heart, is freely offered to anyone who desires it.

Fr. Mateo, the founder and spiritual father of the enthronement movement, would often share that we needed to create in our hearts another Bethany. By this he meant a place where Jesus feels welcome not simply as a king, for whom we run about and try to make the best impression, but as a true friend. A friend listens, a friend shares, and a friend shows love and support in the good times and bad. A true friend doesn't leave when times get hard but rather enters into the messy moments of life, to experience what is truly taking place. Jesus wants to be a friend who knows he is loved and cared for since he loves and cares for us, no matter what.

Fr. Mateo once shared a powerful story of a family who lost everything in a terrible earthquake. He said,

> I went in search of a family where I had enthroned the Sacred Heart and I found my friends quietly standing amidst the smoking ruins of their house while the earth was still quaking. "Father, we have lost everything," the mother said to me, "everything except the peace and happiness which you spoke on the day of the Enthronement. Bethany can never die, for its soul, its peace and its happiness is Jesus."[2]

This awe-inspiring story is rooted in the virtue of hope. Hope is the theological virtue by which we desire the kingdom of heaven and eternal life as our happiness, placing our trust in Christ's promises and relying not on our own strength but on the help of the grace of the Holy Spirit (CCC, 1817).

No matter how difficult life might seem, we cannot allow the world to steal our inner peace, rob us of our hope, and cause us to despair. The powerful words "Bethany can never die . . . its peace and its happiness is Jesus," ring true.[3] Jesus is the reason for our joy. He is our greatest gift, and he desires to live with us within our ordinary lives. A devotion to him has the ability to change our view of everything.

St. Margaret Mary once said, "He is more precious than all his gifts. But of these gifts that of his pure love surpasses all others. Alone it should take possession of us, make us work and make us suffer. For it never lets a heart rest."[4] We need to seek him and not allow the things of this world to distract us from receiving his most powerful love.

When we are in union with Jesus, we can endure the most difficult moments of life. We are reminded in the Gospel of Matthew, "Seek first the kingdom of God and his righteousness, and all these things will be given you besides" (Mt 6:33). When we seek first the kingdom of God, we direct our time, talent, and resources toward his kingdom and learn what it means to have a Christ-centered life. Jesus doesn't promise that we will not have to carry crosses. Rather, he promises that he will strengthen us in order to accomplish our tasks and reward us for our faithfulness.

If we allow Jesus to be our shelter in times of trouble, he will literally hide us from our enemies and protect us. "For God will hide me in his shelter in time of trouble, He will conceal me in the cover of his tent; and set me high upon a rock"(Ps 27:5). Jesus' heart is the perfect place to hide, to find renewal and restoration, and to receive the graces we need. Jesus desires to be our stronghold, and he will be if we allow it.

PONDERING THE PROMISE

Do not allow anxiety, worry, and stress to prevent you from praying and discovering this powerful promise. In life it is easy to be so busy or consumed by the worries of the day that you forget to pray. Shut your eyes and ask Jesus to show you how much he loves you and how he can be your refuge. Then ponder the following:

1. Do you believe that the Lord is offering you secure refuge in life and death? What does that mean to you? Do you desire to be in full communion with the Church? Do you desire and pray for a holy death, and how do you live for that end? This question causes us to ponder how the Lord is offering us refuge.
2. How do you deal with life and death? How do you pray for those who have died before you? Do you believe in the resurrection of the body? Do you believe you will see your loved ones again?
3. "Seek first the kingdom of God and his righteousness, and all these things will be given you besides" (Mt 6:33). How do you see a connection between seeking the kingdom of God and allowing Jesus to

be your refuge? How can you grow in this area of your life?

PRAYING THE PROMISE

As mentioned earlier, the following prayer was a great grace in the life of my extended family. I love the way it covers every aspect of life and sets up a structure for how we are to interact with our Lord. In it we praise him and entrust ourselves to his care in all matters important to us. If we take this approach to our relationship with Jesus, we will be cared for just as so many more who have gone before us have been.

A PRAYER FOR MYSELF

O most holy Heart of Jesus, fountain of every blessing,

I adore you, I love you and will a lively sorrow for my sins.

I offer you this poor heart of mine.

Make me humble, patient, pure, and wholly obedient to your will.

Grant, good Jesus, that I may live in you and for you.

Protect me in the midst of danger; comfort me in my afflictions;

give me health of body, assistance in my temporal needs,

your blessings on all that I do, and the grace of a holy death.

Within your heart I place my every care.

In every need let me come to you with humble trust saying,

Heart of Jesus, help me.

Amen.[5]

PRACTICING THE PROMISE

The year I studied abroad in college I was eating lunch at a restaurant in Austria when I encountered my first *Herrgottswinkel*, or prayer corner. I was immediately drawn to the Crucifix and images of the Sacred Heart and the Immaculate Heart of Mary tucked into an out-of-the-way nook in the establishment. These displays are part of European culture, especially in Austria and Germany. Sometimes they are referred to as the "eye of God," since they are meant as a place not only to gather and pray but also to remind us that the Lord is here with us, "our unseen guest" at the dinner table or family gathering.

Would you like having a dedicated spot in a special room where you can pray? Consider creating a prayer corner in your home or office, someplace where you can go to respond to the great call to prayer. What might you need? A crucifix, a comfortable chair or kneeler, a Bible and other great spiritual books, a Sacred Heart image (we know we will be blessed if we pray before the image), blessed medallions, a beautiful set of rosary beads, and a vial of holy water can all be useful in helping you create the perfect spot. Why not ask the Lord and his Blessed Mother to guide you to the items you need to create a place to take refuge and draw nearer to the Lord?

Take a few minutes now to offer the Litany of the Sacred Heart of Jesus.

5

Recognize Jesus' Blessing and Guidance

Promise #5

I will bestow abundant blessings upon all their undertakings.

The Sacred Heart of Jesus Christ gives you these holy aspirations through the ardent love He bears you, which makes him desire to possess your heart whole and entire.

—St. Margaret Mary[1]

Many families and individuals who choose to enthrone the Sacred Heart of Jesus in their homes share that one way the Lord affirmed their decision was by granting new blessings on their undertakings. Their newfound devotion to the Sacred Heart inspired them to action as the Holy Spirit gave them the strength and direction they needed to act. As time went on, their faith became a higher priority and caused them to see God in all things.

I experienced a powerful "reset" after our family did the enthronement to the Sacred Heart after purchasing our current house in 2013. Shortly after this powerful ceremony took place in our home, I was asked to speak at my first conference, and in a few short years I have been blessed to become a national speaker, an author, and a promoter of the Sacred Heart. Over the last few years, the Lord has invited me to serve him and opened many doors to make it possible. He has also given my husband and me many graces to embrace our marriage vocation and to raise a large Catholic family.

Once, while praying at the end of Mass for direction, I saw a lightning bolt of fire jump out of the Sacred Heart statue's heart and lasso my husband and me. The message of that vision was clear to me; the Sacred Heart desired to protect my marriage and affirm it as the primary means of doing the will of God in my life. I couldn't do ministry work without these special graces helping me to balance a healthy family life.

Jesus doesn't want to be kept in a "Sunday morning box." He desires to bless and help us each day to find new meaning in all aspects of life: our careers, family lives, hobbies, and relationships. This is one reason many organizations choose to welcome the Sacred Heart of Jesus into their school, business, or ministry.

I experienced a similar sense of God's direction, to serve as the director of the Sacred Heart Enthronement Network, the first time I prayed with a family after leading the home enthronement. I experienced such warmth in my heart, and I knew it was God's way to show me that this is where he wants me to serve him. Of course, this isn't the only way God calls people—sometimes the Lord steps into our lives and gives us a powerful sign of what he wants us to do, while at other times, we are called to trust him and remain faithful in what we think is best. But I will always be grateful that the Lord gave me this sign of blessing as I took up this particular undertaking.

EXPLORING THE PROMISE

This promise of blessings in all our undertakings is not a guarantee that we will be showered with wealth and public recognition just because we say we believe in Christ or practice a particular devotion. Rather, this promise is rooted in the fact that God the Creator of the universe, in his infinite wisdom, ordered things in such a way that the natural outcome of following his precepts will result in goodness. Everything may not turn out perfectly as we planned, for free will allows us to choose wrongly and throw a wrench in the works. However, if we strive to do what is right, we can expect the best possible outcome. In this way, this promise is all about trusting in the Lord, seeking his guidance with the intent of conforming our will to his, and then not being afraid to act.

As Christians, we are called not only to live a life of prayer but also to trust that the Lord is leading us in all that we do and to build the kingdom of God here on earth. Fr. Stash Dailey, spiritual director of the national Sacred Heart Enthronement Network and Sacred Heart

Columbus, decided to start witnessing enthronements to the Sacred Heart early in his priesthood because he didn't know how else to help needy families and individuals in his parish. The needs were so great and so complex, he knew they needed Jesus more than anything else. This small step of faith began with a desire to help a few families, and now, in less than ten years, thousands of families have been touched by his work.

Jesus wants us to bring the kingdom of God here on earth. He "equips the called," asking us to trust in him and then step out in faith and see where it leads. Jesus tells us, "It was not you who chose me, but I who chose you and appointed you to go and bear fruit that will remain, so that whatever you ask the Father *in my name* he may give you" (Jn 15:16; emphasis added). Notice that he promises we will receive blessings for what we do *in his name*, that is, with humility and the intention of advancing God's agenda, not our own.

St. Margaret Mary urges us, "Work courageously and untiringly in the vineyard of the Lord, for this is the price of your crown; you just forget yourself and all your own interests and think only of increasing his glory in the work He has confided to you."[2] When we do this, Philippians reminds us that "my God will fully supply whatever you need, in accord with his glorious riches in Christ Jesus" (Phil 4:19).

PONDERING THE PROMISE

Take a few minutes and allow your mind to ponder this promise given by Jesus to St. Margaret Mary. Slow your breathing, bow your head, and pray with your heart. It is so easy to be overwhelmed and anxious about our our lives, our families, and our work, and this stress can prevent us from seeking the Lord's blessing and guidance. Once you have quietened your heart, take a few moments to ponder the following:

1. Are you willing to surrender your life to the Sacred Heart and receive this powerful blessing? If not, what is holding you back?
2. What would "abundant blessing" look like in your life? Where do you need help right now? Is it with your family? Your job? Your career? Your ministry? In what aspect of your life do you need Jesus to turn tables upside down and set your life right-side-up?
3. Do you look for the face of Christ in your daily life, and allow Jesus to lead you in all aspects of your life? "My God will fully supply whatever you need, in accord with his glorious riches in Christ Jesus" (Phil 4:19).

PRAYING THE PROMISE

The Beatitudes (see Matthew 5:3–12) provide the perfect ladder leading to perfection and helping us connect prayer with service. I can still recall being at the Church of the Beatitudes near the Sea of Galilee and reflecting on what my life would be like if I were able to live the Beatitudes out in their fullness. Jesus offers us a path to holiness that is like nothing the world can comprehend, and yet this is where we will find true peace, joy, comfort, and blessing.

Let us slowly read the Beatitudes and ask the Holy Spirit to give us spiritual insight and a greater desire to grow in holiness.

THE BEATITUDES

Blessed are the poor in spirit,
for theirs is the kingdom of heaven.
Blessed are they who mourn,
for they will be comforted.
Blessed are the meek,
for they will inherit the land.
Blessed are they who hunger and thirst for righteousness,
for they will be satisfied.
Blessed are the merciful,
for they will be shown mercy.
Blessed are the clean of heart,
for they will see God.
Blessed are the peacemakers,
for they will be called children of God.
Blessed are they who are persecuted for the sake of righteousness,
for theirs is the kingdom of heaven.
Blessed are you when they insult you and persecute you and utter every kind of evil against you [falsely] because of me. Rejoice and be glad, for your reward will be great in heaven. (Mt 5:3–12)

Amen.

PRACTICING THE PROMISE

As children we were taught, "Say your prayers before bed." Making an examination of conscience is a good way to begin: take a moment to assess your day, reflect on your actions, consider how you have fallen short of the mark, and assert your desire to do better tomorrow. Recall the blessings you received throughout your day, including the ways God may have answered your prayers. (Remember that some of God's greatest gifts in our lives are unanswered prayers.)

Taking time to review your day with God is a great way to become more mindful of how he is working in your life each day. It fosters a sense of gratitude, which is an essential element of forming our will to God's and receiving his blessings.

Once you have completed your examen, conclude by offering the Litany of the Sacred Heart of Jesus.

6

Accept Jesus' Mercy and Show Mercy to Others

Promise #6

Sinners will find in my heart the source and infinite ocean of mercy.

> In his Divine Heart, which is like a bottomless abyss, He revealed to me the treasures of love and grace He has reserved for those who devote themselves to glorifying his Sacred Heart according to their capacity.
>
> —St. Margaret Mary[1]

I was first introduced to the concept of God's mercy by praying the Divine Mercy chaplet with my parents, who would often express God's love to me as we sat and prayed together as a family. Before we began the prayers, we would always go from person to person and apologize for anything we had done to offend another family member; most of the time we would receive mercy and forgiveness from them in return. This small act was more than an offering of kindness; it was a way of forming our souls in the mercy of God and living a life of virtue.

As a youth, this powerful prayer became one of the mainstays of my spirituality, and it is still where I go in times of need. The first book I wrote with my friend, Michele Faehnle, was *Divine Mercy for Moms*. In that book, I share how this devotion touched my heart and helped me to understand that the Lord desires to be merciful toward me and is always inviting me back into his loving embrace. No matter what we do, the Lord offers us his mercy and love.

Now that I am a wife and parent, I see the Divine Mercy devotion as a beautiful gift for my own family. I want my children to know that the Lord is offering his merciful love to them at all times, freeing them from baggage and pain. Sin drags us down, so when we forgive and show others this type of compassion, we are set free.

EXPLORING THE PROMISE

This sixth promise of Jesus to St. Margaret Mary brings Divine Mercy and the Sacred Heart together in one powerful, unified message. For some, these two devotions might be misunderstood as "dueling devotions," and yet nothing could be further from the truth. In fact, they complement one another: each of them contains the same basic message, tailored to suit the needs of the times in which they were delivered.

> The Marian Fathers shared that when we look at the Image of the Merciful Savior (in the Divine Mercy image), we see rays of Blood and Water emanating from the area of his pierced Heart. The rays are emanating outward—they are going out to a hurting world. That is perhaps one of the differences; the Sacred Heart enables us to get a deeper understanding of the infinite mercy and calls us to reparation, yet the Divine Mercy now calls us to live that message to a hurting world.[2]

Through both of these devotions, we encounter the mercy that flows from the heart of Jesus, his most Sacred Heart, and learn that mercy is endless and available to anyone who asks for it. Further, we are to be disciples of mercy and help spread Christ's mercy to others.

Jesus professed that "the Son of Man has come to seek and to save what was lost" (Lk 19:10). The greatest desire of Christ the Good Shepherd is the return of his lost sheep. He came to save the lost and to set up his kingdom throughout the world, embracing all cultures and nationalities. "'I desire mercy, not sacrifice.' I did not come to call the righteous but sinners" (Mt 9:13).

Fr. Mateo, the father of enthronement, defined mercy as "unspeakable condescension of him who is infinite sanctity and justice; condescension favoring in a special way the sick, the wretched, the guilty, the ungrateful, the executioners of God."[3] St. Margaret Mary shared that Jesus said, "Fear not, it is I, Jesus which means Savior. I have come to remind you that the love that fills my Heart is a merciful love. I have come for sinners. I reveal my Heart especially to sinners, that they may all be converted. Sinners will find in my Heart a boundless ocean of mercy. Therefore, I ask you to trust me . . . blindly . . . with childlike trust."[4]

As Catholic Christians, we must all recognize that we are sinners and that Jesus came to save us. When we come to this powerful understanding, we no longer judge others or place blame; instead we begin to look for ways to live as Christians and to spread the message of God's merciful love.

In her famous *Diary*, St. Faustina recounts three ways that Christ wants us to show mercy to others. "**I am giving you three ways of exercising mercy toward your neighbor: the first—by deed, the second—by word, the third—by prayer. In these three degrees is contained the fullness of mercy, and it is an unquestionable proof of love for me. By this means a soul glorifies and pays reverence to my mercy.**"[5]

Years ago when I first read this passage, I instantly connected with this image of mercy. It gave me a clear path to follow in order to cultivate a more merciful heart and share mercy with others. What I discovered is that I can always respond to those in need, even if only through a simple deed, a kind word, or a sincere prayer. When we act merciful toward our neighbors, we mirror Christ to others. When I started to live this "merciful formula," I started to see growth in my marriage and in my relationships. I started to see pride melt away, and forgiveness became easier to impart.

The Sacred Heart of Jesus is where the merciful rays shine out to all. May we seek to not only love his holy heart but also share mercy with others.

PONDERING THE PROMISE

We live in a society where mercy and forgiveness are often not valued. In the news, people are defined by the mistakes they make. In one instant they are celebrities living a life of fame and popularity, and the next they are abandoned over something they say or do. Mercy is not a concept that is easily accepted, as it is hard to be merciful to a person who is "undeserving" of a second chance. As a friend once said, "We destroy people with our tongues and don't think twice." Mercy begins with a change of heart.

Jesus doesn't want us to fear him and run in the opposite direction when we sin; rather, he is always waiting for us with loving arms, inviting us to return to his embrace. Spend a minute reflecting on the story of the prodigal son who returns home to the father (see Luke 15:11–32). The son wasted his father's money and even spent his inheritance as if his father were dead. While this son was wasteful and sinful, he eventually realized his life at home was better than the life he had in a foreign land tending to the pigs. However, the older son lacked the mercy the father was offering, and this left him cold and bitter.

Without mercy, our hearts grow cold and judgmental. We cannot get past what we believe the other person deserves—typically pure justice, and yet, we never want that standard for us. This gospel story is full of powerful messages. Spend a few minutes thinking about it from the viewpoint of all three characters. Then consider how you would answer the following questions about your own life.

1. Do you have a hard time accepting that the Lord is offering you his mercy and desires that we express mercy to others? How can we show mercy to those with whom we struggle?
2. St. Margaret Mary said, "In his divine Heart, which is like a bottomless abyss, He revealed to me the treasures of love and grace He has reserved for those who devote themselves to glorifying his Sacred Heart according to their capacity."[6] The essential phrase of this line is "capacity." Let us not hold others to *our* standards but rather show them love and compassion and recognize that the Lord is seeking everyone.
3. When we read in Hebrews 4:16 "So let us confidently approach the throne of grace to receive mercy and to find grace for timely help," we learn that our Lord wants to help us. Have you called upon his mercy in your prayer life for yourself and others?

PRAYING THE PROMISE

Let us take a minute to pause and pray this powerful prayer to allow the Mercy of God to penetrate our own hearts and make us willing to extend this mercy out to others. Jesus desires to set us free from our past sins and hurts. When we experience God's merciful love, like the Prodigal Son, we can be healed and restored as a son or daughter of the Lord. May the broken and wounded heart of our Lord reach our very souls and heal us so that we can go forth and love others and be vessels of mercy.

PRAYER FOR MERCY

Behold, O compassionate Father, this prodigal who has sinned against Thee by scattering the treasures with which Thou hast enriched me. I throw myself at Thy Feet and cry for mercy. Do not reject me and do not forget Thy mercies. Exercise them over my poor soul, although it is unworthy of them. Do not permit that it be lost before Thine eyes, since Thy Sacred Heart has given birth to it with so much pain. Do not refuse me the title of child of Thy Heart, for I desire to die unto myself and unto sin, in order to live henceforth only by the life of submission and obedience. In this spirit I wish to do all my actions, uniting my obedience with that which Thou dost render to the priest, whether he be good or bad, without showing the pain it costs Thee to enter into the hearts of sinners. In like manner, I will repress my repugnance so that they will have no other effect on me but to make me sacrifice them to Thee, saying: Jesus was silent; Jesus was obedient even unto death; I wish to obey until I breathe my last sigh.

Amen.

Lord, have Mercy on me, a sinner.[7]

PRACTICING THE PROMISE

Begin by evaluating what deeds, words, and prayers you can offer to others in need: How can I alleviate someone's suffering? Can I bring a meal, send a card, say a kind word, or just offer a simple prayer on behalf of another? Perhaps a donation of treasure or talent to the poor or a special charity? Now, pick one and resolve to carry it out. Make an intentional plan and follow through with it.

Take a moment now and offer the Litany of the Sacred Heart of Jesus.

7

PRAY TO BE SET ON FIRE WITH THE LOVE OF CHRIST

Promise #7

Lukewarm souls shall become fervent.

> Bring to this divine Heart all your troubles and affections, for whatever emanates (comes) from the Sacred Heart is sweet; it changes everything into love.
>
> —St. Margaret Mary[1]

During the early years of marriage, I had a house full of children, and my "yes to life" had me feeling burned out and exhausted. Having been raised in the faith, I knew that God had graces to offer me; I just didn't really know how to plug in and start accessing them in a way that would make them real in my life.

The scripture passage that provided me the most consolation during that time in my life was "Come to me, all you who labor and are burdened, and I will give you rest. Take my yoke upon you and learn from me, for I am meek and humble of heart; and you will find rest for yourselves. For my yoke is easy, and my burden light" (Mt 11:28–30).

I began my search for relief from the burdens that had been weighing me down by making slight changes in my spiritual life. I started to reprioritize my schedule so that I had time to pray more, could go to confession on a regular basis, and could spend more time simply resting in the presence of the Lord. I started being more sincere with myself and with God, opening up with Jesus about how I was feeling and trying to be a more authentic person. Over time, I discovered that even my prayers began to change; I started to ask him not just for the material things I needed but also to soften my heart and change *me*. I was ready for my "heart transplant."

As my prayer life deepened, I began to experience a great desire to go to Mass more frequently and receive the Holy Eucharist, and once more I began tweaking my schedule to make time for daily Mass. These daily encounters with grace provided me the strength to embrace my vocation as a path to holiness and offer all of my trials up to Jesus.

EXPLORING THE PROMISE

Sometimes challenging moments can awaken the soul and remind us what it means to truly live. Thankfully, God can use all things to wake us up and remind us of the loving relationship he is offering us. The Bible tells us, "We know that all things work for good for those who love God, who are called according to his purpose" (Rom 8:28). The Sacred Heart devotion is a reminder that our Lord is always offering us his holy heart and life experiences that can awaken our heart. Jesus can take our pains, sufferings, illness, and brokenness and use them to bring out a greater glory. Perhaps the greatest example is how Jesus won our redemption by his death on the Cross.

St. Claude de la Colombiere exclaims, "If men knew how pleasing this devotion is to Jesus, there is no Christian—however lukewarm they might be—who would not at once practice it. Urge souls, and more especially those serving God and religion, to consecrate themselves to the Sacred Heart."[2]

When we choose to consecrate ourselves to Jesus' Sacred Heart, we leave room for his heart to transform our lives. If we become bored, if our hearts grow numb and unable to respond, this can cause us great trouble. "I know your works; I know that you are neither cold nor hot. I wish you were either cold or hot. So, because you are lukewarm, neither hot nor cold, I will spit you out of my mouth" (Rv 3:15–16). On the other hand, when we draw close to his Sacred Heart and experience the almighty love of God, transformation is possible, and our lukewarm souls can become fervent.

As we know, our culture today largely suffers from this apathetic response to faith. And yet the Lord is *always* knocking on our hearts, *always* inviting us into a love relationship that is far from boring or apathetic. He invites us to know him, love him, and serve him. Jesus is always inviting us—every minute of our lives—but it is our decision to respond. He initiates all communication, and it is our job to respond. This is the hope, the solution to our indifferent ways.

Pope Francis recently tweeted, "There are two attitudes typical of lukewarm Christians: putting God in a corner—either you do this for me or I won't go to Church anymore—and washing our hands of those in need. Let us get rid of these attitudes to make space for the Lord who is coming. #HomilySantaMarta"[3]

Our Lord is knocking on your heart and wants to come in. This great call never ceases, so it is never too late to respond. The Sacred Heart desires a heart response to his calling, a heart reawakened with the flames of the Sacred Heart. He is longing to be invited into your heart and home, desiring to dine with your friends. Be earnest, therefore, and repent. We read, "Behold, I stand at the door and knock. If anyone hears my voice and opens the door, [then] I will enter his house and dine with him, and he with me" (Rv 3:20).

Fr. Francis Larkin once wrote that the Sacred Heart devotion through enthronement to the Sacred Heart is designed to "help the family to come alive with the spirit of faith, love and reverence, . . . aiding the family to becoming in truth a 'domestic sanctuary' of charity."[4] Addressing Fr. Mateo Crawley-Boevey, Pope Paul XI wrote in a letter, "You do well, beloved son, to take up the cause of human society, by first stirring up and spreading the Christian spirit in families and homes, and by establishing in the center of our families the love of Jesus Christ to reign and rule there."[5]

PONDERING THE PROMISE

Allow the Lord to speak to your heart. When you give the Lord permission to act in your life, you can experience his power and grace. Jesus needs your free-will consent to draw you deeper in relationship with him. When you seek out solace in the heart of Jesus, he helps you discover him in new ways. He wants you to come to know him as the great King of love. Now ask yourself:

1. Do you see this devotion to the Sacred Heart as a way to grow in your faith and become more passionate or enthusiastic? How can you and your family grow closer to Christ through deepening your prayer life?
2. What does "lukewarm" look like in your life? Ask Jesus to speak to your heart and share with you how to break the bonds of apathy, indifference, and coldness.
3. "Behold, I stand at the door and knock. If anyone hears my voice and opens the door, [then] I will enter his house and dine with him, and he with me" (Rv 3:20). Jesus is knocking; every moment he calls us and desires that we open the door to the King of love. How is this scripture speaking to you?

PRAYING THE PROMISE

Now, let us pray that our hearts will be set on fire with the love of Christ and that our devotion for the Sacred Heart of Jesus will become and remain fervent.

PRAYER FOR MERCY

Lord Jesus, so passionately in love with men that you can no longer hold the flames of that burning love; let that love spread abroad by means of me. Reveal yourself to men through me and enrich them with your profound treasures, which hold all the graces they need to be saved and sanctified. Amen.[6]

PRACTICING THE PROMISE

Resolve to complete fifteen minutes of prayer a day before your image of the Sacred Heart, and invite the Blessed Mother to lead you to Jesus. Mary, the Mother of God, always points you to Jesus, and Jesus shares his mother with you. As Mary was the first to hear his tiny heartbeat as a young child, she too wants you to grow close to his loving heart.

Marian devotion is closely linked with the Sacred Heart devotion. So when you spend time in prayer before your image, invite the Blessed Mother to join you through prayers like the Rosary, and ask her—the sinless, Immaculate Heart—to strengthen you and help you, as any good mother would.

Consider what it would take to make prayer a priority, to truly pray each day for your loved ones, for your country, or for the intention of the Holy Father. The more you pray, the more you will appreciate this time.

Try setting your alarm forward fifteen minutes and allow the Lord to be with you in the morning, or choose another time and set a reminder on your phone or smartwatch so you won't forget. It has been said that our calendars reflect our priorities. Why not use yours to schedule a special time for prayer?

Instead of cursing the times when you can't sleep, use those times instead as a way of giving the Lord all twenty-four hours of your day, seven days a week, and welcome him even into your night hours. Fr. Stash Dailey once said, "Devotion to the Sacred Heart of Jesus begins when we stop cursing the Name of Jesus and invoke a friendship with him."[7]

Think about what prayers you will say. Perhaps read the daily readings and then reflect on them. Include some time to offer up your intentions to God. Speak to him as you would a dear friend, and share what is in the depths of your heart.

Take a moment now to offer the Litany of the Sacred Heart.

8

SEEK CHRIST'S PERFECTION BY PRAYING AND FASTING

Promise #8

Fervent souls shall quickly mount to high perfection.

> Father Croiset once said that all the saints of the Church who have been flooded with the greatest graces have had a most tender and intimate love for Jesus, and also that there are few who have not loved the wounded Heart of Jesus with a most tender devotion.
>
> —Rev. Dr. Joseph Keller, *The Sacred Heart*[1]

On his seventy-fifth birthday, my grandfather received a very special gift: a birthday letter from Mother Teresa (now St. Teresa of Calcutta), thanking him for years of service to the Sacred Heart of Jesus. This letter arrived by mail from India and was hand typed with the simple signature at the bottom. It read, "God loves you for all your devoted service in spreading his Kingdom on earth."

This was one of the most surprising moments for me as a youth, for it wasn't until that moment that I realized what an extraordinary man my grandfather was. What had he done to deserve a letter from such a great world leader and future saint? Why had she taken time out of her work, feeding and caring for the poorest of the poor, to remember my grandpa, a simple man who lived in Cincinnati, Ohio?

In time, I discovered the truth of it all: This unpretentious, meek, elderly man was not by worldly standards a remarkable person, yet he had helped to feed tens of thousands of souls through his work promoting the devotion to the Sacred Heart. After he retired from working second shift at Ford Motor Company as a tool and die maker, he went to work full-time for the kingdom of God. He started to make plaques with the images of the Sacred Heart of Jesus and Immaculate Heart of Mary out of his basement workshop. He and a group of friends from the Men of the Sacred Hearts Center in Cincinnati shipped more than twenty thousand of them to the Missionaries of Charity!

For years, he cut, glued, and prepared these images to be shipped around the world. On the backs of the plaques were the promises of the Sacred Heart and the promises of the Rosary, to give people a holy incentive to promote this devotion and to live a life of prayer. These simple images were placed in homes of the poor, the sick, and the dying throughout India, Albania, and beyond. To this day they are still called "Art Plaques" since my grandpa's name was Arthur.

In another letter, dated December 7, 1991, Mother Teresa wrote, "Our poor people are also grateful to you for the pictures they are able to put up in their homes to show their devotion to the Sacred Heart and honor him. . . . Thank you for the love and devotion you have for the Sacred Heart of Jesus and the great zeal you have for spreading this devotion all over the world. You are a consolation to his Heart at a time when so many are wounding him."

Only recently did I discovered that these images had found their way all across the United States as well. About six years ago, while touring a house we were considering buying, I walked into one of the children's bedroom and saw an "Art Plaque" on the wall! The mother who lived there said, "They were a first communion gift from the local Catholic school. All my children have them." Imagine my shock and joy at seeing the images my grandfather had created in the home of a stranger, nearly ten years after his death.

EXPLORING THE PROMISE

Countless examples exist of ordinary people such as my grandfather receiving sanctification through this powerful devotion, some of whom have since been canonized as Catholic saints. Saints are ordinary people who die and are remembered for outstanding holiness.

In the introduction, we read about St. Margaret Mary, the Great Apostle of the Sacred Heart, as well as St. Gertrude the Great. These women both had such a deep and profound understanding that this devotion leads to high perfection, but they were not alone. Included below are some powerful quotations by some saints about how they saw this devotion come alive in their lives:

St. Madeleine Sophie Barat (1779–1865) founded the Society of the Sacred Heart in 1800. The purpose of this society was to make known the love of God revealed in the heart of Christ and take part in the restoration of Christian life in France through the education of young women, rich or poor. St. Madeleine once said, "Christ does not ask that we become perfect all at once, but that we work towards this each day, in the measure that grace operates in us and the radiance of the Holy Spirit enlightens us."[2]

St. Margaret Mary Alacoque (1647–1690) said, "This devotion is as a last effort of his love . . . to favor men in these last centuries with this loving redemption, in order to withdraw them from the empire of Satan, which he intends to destroy, and in order to put them under the sweet empire of his love and thus bring many souls by his saving grace to the way of eternal salvation." [3]

St. Alphonsus Liguori (1696–1787) founded the Redemptorist order of priests, a congregation dedicated to providing parish missions, especially to the poor in rural areas. He encouraged an intimate, personal relationship with Jesus Christ through frequent visits to the Blessed Sacrament and was devoted to the Sacred Heart of Jesus as a sign and symbol of Christ's love. In his writings, St. Alphonsus stated, "To advance in the way of holiness it is necessary above all else to concentrate one's efforts on loving God. God's infinite majesty certainly deserves all our reverence and submission, but He himself prefers to receive from souls desirous of loving him their love and confidence rather than fear and servility."[4]

St. Frances Cabrini (1850–1919) founded the Institute of the Missionary Sisters of the Sacred Heart of Jesus in 1880, and in 1889 came to New York to organize catechism and education classes for Italian immigrants and provide for the needs of orphans. Her prayer to the Sacred Heart was, "My Jesus, I have not always recognized your loving plans for me. Every day, with the help of your light, I learn more of your loving care. Continue to increase my awareness of the gentleness of your loving plans."[5]

St. Thérèse of Lisieux (1873–1897) said, "Pray to the Sacred Heart; You know that I myself do not see the Sacred Heart as everybody else. I think that the heart of my spouse is mine alone, just as mine is his alone, and I speak to him then in the solitude of this delightful heart to heart, while waiting to contemplate him one day face to face."[6]

St. John Paul II (1920–2005) said, "In the Sacred Heart every treasure of wisdom and knowledge is hidden. In that Divine Heart beats God's infinite love for everyone, for each one of us individually."[7]

These powerful saint quotations are beautiful reminders that living out a devotion to the Sacred Heart is an invitation to grow in holiness and to be transformed into fervent souls seeking perfection in Christ.

PONDERING THE PROMISE

Christ invites us to strive to be like him. He wants to purify us and lead us on the road to perfection—not the perfection of the world, such as beauty or style, but the perfection of holiness. Attaining such perfection is a great deal of work, but as my grandfather Art used to quip, "The pay is out of this world." Now consider for a moment:

1. St. Margaret Mary warned, "This devotion is as a last effort of his love . . . to favor men in these last centuries with this loving redemption, in order to withdraw them from the empire of Satan, which He intends to destroy, and in order to put them under the sweet empire of his love and thus bring many souls by his saving grace to the way of eternal salvation."[8] What does this suggest about the connection between living out a devotion to the Sacred Heart and our hope of spending eternity with God in heaven?
2. What does it mean to "imitate Christ" through this act of consecration to the Sacred Heart?
3. Which of the saint quotations touched your heart? Reread the list slowly, and spend some time pondering how these holy saints benefited from this powerful devotion.

PRAYING THE PROMISE

Let us pause from the busyness of life and ponder the transformation that is possible with the help of our Lord from lukewarm to fervent to perfection. How can we seek to grow closer to Christ today, in this very moment? Offer up a prayer from your heart, or recite the one below, sharing with Jesus your great desire for transformation. Seek his grace in areas that have you stressed and anxious. Give all that you have to God.

PRAYER OF TRUST TO THE SACRED HEART

Holy Heart of Jesus, Sweet Sanctuary of rest,
bring peace to my soul and settle my spirit,
especially in the matter of ____.
Here, I place all of my worries and fears
into the wound of your Sacred Heart,
to be tended to in accordance with your perfect will,
which desires only the best and highest good.
Your love alone is enough, and I surrender to it;
clinging with hope, trust, and confidence in all of your promises.
Amen.

PRACTICING THE PROMISE

When you take time out to pray, fast, and give to others, you are being like Christ. Seek Christ and embrace your faith through deepening your prayer life and fasting from the pleasures of the world so you can more clearly see the Lord in your life. St. Augustine writes, "Do you wish your prayer to reach God? Give it two wings, fasting and almsgiving."[9]

You might begin to take the first steps toward fasting by saying yes to God, and no to small pleasures throughout your day. What can you do to begin to offer up small acts of fasting? Could you fast on Fridays? Is there a pleasure, such as social media viewing, watching movies or shows for pleasure, or sugar in your coffee, that you can refrain from out of love of God?

When you start fasting, you will discover the gift of freedom by choosing to offer these things up on behalf of your love of God. You will slowly realize that these pleasures don't have bondage over you, that you don't *need* your coffee, wine, chocolate, tech time, drive-through cheeseburger, or candy. When you take steps to being intentional about your actions, you gain a new perspective on your life.

Take a moment now to offer the Litany of the Sacred Heart of Jesus.

9

DEDICATE YOUR HOME (AND SCHOOL AND WORKPLACE) TO JESUS

Promise #9

I will bless every place in which an image of my heart is exposed and honored.

> The Sacred Heart of my adorable Master has given me to understand that his desire to be known, loved and honored by men is so excessive that He has promised to all those who consecrate and devote themselves to it in order to give it this pleasure; that He will never allow them to perish.
>
> —St. Margaret Mary,
> *Letters of St. Margaret Mary Alacoque*[1]

A dear friend recently handed me a copy of an article from our local paper that was first printed in 1955 and rediscovered by her family in the late 1970s. The article, titled "Religion Gives Fullness to Life," shared how her family lived out their Catholic faith in their daily lives, including how her family enthroned the Sacred Heart of Jesus in her home.

"We practiced the faith as a family in the 1950s," my friend explained to me.

> We said the Rosary daily, went to Mass each week, and attempted to live virtuous lives. Now, after a long life, I can see the fruits of my parents' faith. No matter what difficulties we have all faced, my siblings and I have all been *offered* the graces we have needed; we simply had to choose to access them. My Catholic faith has been my passion and strength in good and bad times, and my parents' devotion to the Sacred Heart allowed me to embrace this devotion more readily than I might have if I hadn't had their example—if Jesus had not been enthroned as the center of our home.

She thought a moment; then she said to me, "It has been sixty-five years since this article was published in our local paper, and I can say that in all that time I have never been truly alone. Jesus is my house guest, and he is with me always, my unseen guest."

Every family that does the enthronement can typically share one grace, blessing, or insight they received about how the Lord wanted to be invited in to help strengthen the family and lead them closer to his heart. Enthronement to the Sacred Heart of Jesus is a way to help families grow closer to Christ. Through it we become more aware of the need for grace to preserve and protect our family from evil influences and learn how to navigate living in the world. Further, enthronement helps us to see the many amazing opportunities to involve Christ in our careers, lifestyles, activities, schooling, and sports. I can now see that the Sacred Heart wanted to help our family and that Jesus is inviting all families to take this leap in faith of welcoming him as well.

EXPLORING THE PROMISE

> Blessed be the God and Father of our Lord Jesus Christ, who has blessed us in Christ with every spiritual blessing in the heavens.
>
> —Ephesians 1:3

Near the turn of the last century, Fr. Mateo Crawley-Boevey, founder of the Sacred Heart Enthronement movement, said, "The action of Enthroning the Sacred Heart has an impact on families and individuals that carries over to society and becomes the basis for spreading the Social Reign of our King and Savior."[2]

One of the great aspects of enthronement to the Sacred Heart is that it's not just for families and individuals who want to give their hearts and homes to Jesus; enthronement can and should also be done in Catholic schools, businesses, organizations, and parishes. Jesus, the King of love, wants to reign everywhere; this is how we grow our heavenly kingdom here on earth.

Enthronement is a Christian ceremony where the person or persons welcome the King of love to come and rule. When we give Jesus our life, we seek not to compartmentalize our faith but rather to live in a way that honors our Lord in all that we do.

Catholic schools are a perfect place for the enthronement to the Sacred Heart: it reminds all who attend that the school exists primarily to teach its students about Jesus and his love for us. Jesus told the disciples, "Let the children come to me." When we recognize Jesus as king, savior, and friend in our schools, we seek to gather the children into his arms.

As the principal (also a deacon) of the local Catholic high school in my area shared,

> Having the Sacred Heart enthroned in our school (since 2016) has been a very powerful reminder of Jesus' forever presence throughout our campus. The Sacred Heart pictures, images, and statues throughout our building—in all classrooms, offices, locker rooms, and even in our elevators—continues to remind all who enter our school about the greatest gift of Christ's very body, blood, soul, and divinity present in our chapel where we have daily access to adore, pray, and honor. The Sacred Heart enthronement has made a tremendous difference in all we do to enhance the Catholic Church's educational mission and apostolate. We know that Christ, as he promised, is always with us until the end of time.

Businesses and organizations can also benefit greatly from enthronement. One business owner shared that after the enthronement to the Sacred Heart, she decided to enthrone the business, and since then she has seen God at work helping her to make her spa more Christ-centered, while still providing outstanding care to those who come. "I am thankful we were willing to give Christ not only our hearts and home but also the business. Our business is a huge responsibility, and now I see that weight was not for me to carry alone, that I shouldn't become anxious and stressed; rather, I need to allow Jesus to reign at work as well. I look forward to seeing Jesus work in our ordinary moments, not just at home but also at work."

Sacred Heart enthronement offers spiritual food to those in great need. When we choose to enthrone the Sacred Heart in any place, we give all who go there an opportunity to experience the love of God and learn how to grow in holiness right alongside the people connected with that place, our families, fellow students, coworkers, parishioners, and friends.

St. Pius XI wrote in the encyclical *Quas Primas,* "The kingship and empire of Christ have been recognized in the pious custom, practiced by many families, of dedicating themselves to the Sacred Heart of Jesus; not only families have performed this act of dedication, but nations, too, and kingdoms. In fact, the whole of the human race was at the insistence of Pope Leo XIII, in the Holy Year 1900, consecrated to the Divine Heart."[3]

Enthronement is a step in deepening your faith life and knowing that God is God and you are not. By welcoming Jesus as king, we unite ourselves to his reign of love. Jesus doesn't rule with the iron fist of control; rather, he leads us with his blazing heart of love. This love was not meant just for us, a few who embrace his holy heart, but for everyone. As Pope Pius XI shares, "When once men recognize, both in private and in public life, that Christ is King, society will at last receive the great blessings of real liberty, well-ordered discipline, peace and harmony."[4] What greater gift can we give than that of peace and harmony?

Enthronement requires three essential elements.

First, we need to choose freely to welcome Jesus; it is a choice. A time of preparation through prayer helps us to prepare our hearts to accept him and is a symbol of that yes. We read in Isaiah 40:3, "In the wilderness prepare the way of the LORD! Make straight in the wasteland a highway for our God!" This is true with our hearts; we need to prepare for him to come. Fr. Mateo suggests three days or more of prayer preparation, but as with anything in life, the more you put into it, the more you get out of it. Consider adding in the sacrament of confession as well in order to have a clean start. However, do not allow yourself to feel overwhelmed, and trust that Christ will reward us for whatever we can offer.

Second, the family or individual needs to expose a blessed image or statue of the Sacred Heart in a "prevalent place." That means somewhere you will see it! It will not do any good in the far corner of the basement. Instead, choose a place where you can easily see it and will encounter it on a regular basis and be reminded of your commitment to honor him.

Third, we must make a formal act of enthronement. It need not be anything elaborate or time-consuming. Fr. Mateo, the founder of the movement, said that the entire ceremony typically only lasts about fifteen minutes.[5]

Enthronement is the kickoff ceremony or the launching pad, not the finish line. Numerous resources are listed in this book for acquiring materials and instructions on how to carry out the ceremony, so there is no need to worry.

The act of enthronement is a powerful way to change the philosophy of your life or that of your family. We read in St. Paul's Second Letter to the Corinthians,

> Moreover, God is able to make every grace abundant for you, so that in all things, always having all you need, you may have an abundance for every good work. As it is written: "He scatters abroad, he gives to the poor; his righteousness endures forever." The one who supplies seed to the sower and bread for food will supply and multiply your seed and increase the harvest of your righteousness. You are being enriched in every way for all generosity, which through us produces thanksgiving to God." (2 Cor 9:8–11)

God wants to bless us in abundance; all we need to do is to trust and be open to the Holy Spirit. God himself cannot be outdone, and by enthroning Jesus in our homes, we are inviting him to be the head of our homes so we can receive his graces in a new way.

Once we've completed the steps of enthroning our homes to the Sacred Heart, we turn to the task of living out the enthronement. This includes embracing the Sacred Heart as our source of strength, our place of refuge, and seeking the graces he wants to offer no matter what lemons are tossed at us. "But you, LORD, are enthroned forever; your renown is for all generations" (Ps 102:13).

The Lord is enthroned forever, and that is exactly what enthronement is, living this psalm out in the life of our family. When we take time to honor the Lord through enthronement, we are taking the first steps of faith by always keeping our mind on Christ. Consider meditating on his Sacred Heart, saying daily prayers before your image at home, and going to Mass. See the connection between the Holy Eucharist and his heart, and begin to trust, with each aspect of your life, that he will be your strength and refuge. The true goal of enthronement is to have your heart set on fire with the love of Christ and to allow this flame to transform your life and the lives of those around you.

Enthronement is not just an individual consecration or dedication but also a decision to enthrone Jesus as king of your whole family, living and deceased. This powerful reality speaks to the scripture "As for me and my household, we will serve the LORD" (Jos 24:15). When we take time to pray for our family and give our entire life to Christ, and those of our family, we trust in his graces and his ability to seek all those who are lost. Now more than ever before we need to stand before the Lord, begging for his blessings and asking for his graces.

PONDERING THE PROMISE

Do not allow anxiety, worry, and stress to prevent you from praying and discovering this powerful promise. It is easy to be so busy or consumed by the worries of the day that you forget to pray. Shut your eyes and ask

Jesus to show you how much he loves you. In what areas of your life do you need to ask him to be your king? In your home life? Your marriage? Your finances? Your parenting? Invite him into that place. Then take a moment to ponder the following.

1. Do you believe that the Lord is offering you his blessing? What place needs blessing? Your home? What kinds of blessings do you long for?
2. Hanging a picture on the wall is a powerful reminder that we must also learn to honor his heart in word, deed, and prayer. Am I willing to give the Sacred Heart of Jesus a chance to change my life?
3. "Everything is possible to one who has faith" (Mk 9:23). What areas do you need help and hope that change is possible?
4. When have you seen this powerful promise lived out in your life or that of another? The purpose of enthronement is to restore faith. Do you believe this is possible for yourself and your family members? Will you pray for it?

PRAYING THE PROMISE

In the Garden of Gethsemane, as Jesus entered into his Passion, he urged his closest friends to remain with him, to watch and pray. A short time later, when Jesus returned to find them asleep, he shook them awake and said to Peter, "Watch and pray that you may not undergo the test. The spirit is willing but the flesh is weak" (Mk 14:38). Just as Jesus asked the disciples in the Garden to wait with him during his agony, the Lord invites us to wait and watch with him. Here is a powerful prayer to include in your home-adoration before your Sacred Heart image as a reminder that the Lord desires us to come to him with what causes us pain. Jesus longs to know our hearts' desires. We are invited to turn to Jesus with all our cares.

PRAYER FOR ANY NEED

Sacred Heart of Jesus, you have so often presented Your Heart as a sign of constant love between us. With utmost confidence, I point to Your Heart, which You took for love of men in the Incarnation, and know that You will grant me this grace which I ask of You. Amen.[6]

—St. Gertrude the Great, 1301

PRACTICING THE PROMISE

Welcome Jesus into your heart and home through enthronement. Visit welcomehisheart.com to learn more about this powerful practice. Next, consider starting a night adoration hour in your home, a practice that involves praying before your image in your home in the late hours of the night for one hour, at least once a month. This time of prayer provides great consolation from the Lord and is proven to bring many blessings to families and communities.

Fr. Mateo once wrote, "Dear Bethanies, come out with lighted torches to meet Jesus Crucified and prove to him that your house is really his dwelling place."[7] He called Catholics to be with our Lord in the wee hours of the night when sin and darkness seems to be at their worst. This act of home adoration is perfect for those who can't sleep and is a perfect way to offer up our cares and worries to Jesus.

Home adoration is also a powerful way to grow closer to Jesus when you can't get to Mass or adoration. If you are homebound or Mass is suspended in your area, as it was in 2020 from the COVID-19 virus, home adoration is a great way to refocus your home prayer life and see that you can link up your prayers with Masses said around the world. When the Mass isn't prayed publicly, it isn't "canceled." Priests are still saying Holy Mass, so consider praying along with the prayers of the Mass, praying the Holy Rosary before your image, praying the litany of the Sacred Heart of Jesus, reading daily scripture, or just pouring your heart out to the Lord.

Take a moment now to offer the Litany of the Sacred Heart of Jesus.

10

Confess Your Sins and Ask Jesus to Soften Your Heart

Promise #10

I will give to priests the gift of touching the most hardened hearts.

> My divine Master revealed to me that it was his ardent desire to be known, loved, and honored by men. He is eager desire to draw them back from the road of perdition [hell], along which Satan is driving them in countless numbers.
>
> —St. Margaret Mary[1]

Forgive me Father for I have sinned." These are the first words expressed by all Catholics during the Sacrament of Reconciliation. How powerful it is, admitting to be a sinner in need of a Savior! The sins a priest hears can be as simple and innocent as a first-time youth's confession or as serious as a person on their deathbed after being away from the Church their entire adult life.

Confession is a sacrament that sets our souls free from sin and its bondages. This sacrament, administered through a priest, allows us to receive forgiveness and spiritual counsel and provides us the opportunity to do penance to make up for our sins, all under a guarantee of confidentiality. What an amazing source of grace it is!

Recently, my bishop shared during his homily in Mass at the annual Sacred Heart Congress an important lesson he learned from his priest mentor / friend who encouraged him to see that we are called to rejoice when sinners come home. He went on to say that each Christmas or Easter the priest should have one paramount desire: to help bring souls back to confession. He said, "I don't want gifts and candy; I want one juicy sinner to come back to faith through going to confession."

When the bishop shared these comments, many of us laughed, and yet it is so true. The greatest gift is when sinners return to faith, and we should all rejoice along with the saints and angels when a person returns to this sacrament. With the power of God's grace, he can set our hearts anew. The Catholic Church is a place that welcomes sinners and desires all of us to grow closer to Christ through the sacraments.

In order to receive forgiveness, we must begin by asking for it. I have learned through my years of parenting that when a young child is stubborn and refuses to ask for forgiveness, it is oftentimes through the act of a warm hug that the child is coaxed to say the words "I am sorry." Often it is just the same with us. When we know we are loved and our request will not be rejected, it is much easier to proclaim those words to God and others. "If we acknowledge our sins, he is faithful and just and will forgive our sins and cleanse us from every wrongdoing" (1 Jn 1:9). Jesus wants us to develop a life of seeking forgiveness from others and God so we can be cleansed and our hearts purified.

We need not be afraid to go to confession; the priest is there as a representative, appointed by Christ himself, he is an *alter Christus*, another Christ. Jesus made this very clear when he instituted the priesthood, saying, "I will give you the keys to the kingdom of heaven. Whatever you bind on earth shall be bound in heaven; and whatever you loose on earth shall be loosed in heaven" (Mt 16:19). This binding and loosing refers to the authority of the Church to administer forgiveness to those who seek it (see *CCC*, 1443–45).

Fr. Nathan Cromley, a priest with Eagle Eye Ministries, shares, "I have seen this promise come alive in the midst of their vocation because this promise is just as much about the unique calling of the priesthood and how we are called to minister much like a 'father' to so many different types of people. Being a spiritual father is a privilege to serve others and be welcomed into the hardest of moments, of death and dying and the greatest celebrations such as baptisms, First Communions and weddings."

He went on to share that "it truly is a gift to walk through an airport and be addressed as 'Father,' and have someone speak to me directly because of that title. I never take being a priest lightly; I know I am called to share the love of Christ. The priesthood is an opportunity to share the message of Christ everywhere I go."[2]

Such words are particularly reassuring to the lay faithful and remind us of the great gift we have in the priesthood. Yet we must recognize that even the most pious or grace-filled priest can't force us to accept the gifts of grace they offer us from Christ. We are called to allow the message of conversion they deliver to penetrate and soften our hardened hearts to produce hearts like Christ's, full of empathy and compassion for others. As another priest from Michigan said, "I see this promise as a beacon of hope in a society that has lost its sense of moral and Christian ways. Jesus is offering us another means to help become aware of deviant behavior which is so embedded in society and leads to hardheartedness. The Sacred Heart is hope for the true restoration the Lord desires!"[3]

EXPLORING THE PROMISE

While this particular promise may seem to be reserved specifically for priests, it does have implications for the lay faithful as well. It is a promise that the Lord will be with our priests and guide them as they minister. It is also a call to us to trust that our priests are instruments of the Lord—and that those whose lives and ministries are devoted to the Sacred Heart of Christ will receive special graces, helping them to grow in personal holiness and to be fruitful in ministry. St. Margaret Mary wrote,

> My divine savior assured me that those who labor for the salvation of souls will have the art of touching the hardest hearts and will obtain marvelous success, *if they themselves are animated with a tender devotion to his Divine Heart*. He [Christ] will penetrate the most unfeeling hearts by the words of his preachers and faithful friends. He will so pour out the sweet unction of his ardent charity, with such strong and powerful graces on their words, that He will make them like a flaming sword which will cause the most frozen hearts to melt in his love. The words of these apostles will be like two-edged swords, which will penetrate the most hardened hearts and make the fountain of penance spring up in them, purifying and sanctifying the most obstinate sinners and rendering them susceptible to the love of this divine Heart. By this means the most criminal souls will be led on to salutary penance.[4]

More than ever before, our society needs the Sacred Heart to warm up hearts and to eliminate interior moral dysfunction. Sin has penetrated all sectors of society, and the devil is primed to spread lies and distortion, which have become almost cultural norms. With the help of technology, we have the potential to do great good and share Christ's message with others, and yet, with a few swipes or clicks, we are able to access sinful images and messages. Sin leads to the hardening of the heart, distorting the dignity of others, causing hearts to grow cold, and dulling compassion and charity.

However, we need not despair, for as the prophet Ezekiel declared to the house of Israel, the Lord does not abandon his people in their impurity but restores them in goodness and truth. "I will give you a new heart, and a new spirit I will put within you. And I will remove the heart of stone from your flesh and give you a heart of flesh" (Ez 36:26).

In establishing the priesthood under the New Covenant, Christ provides the means to guide his people to goodness and truth once more. Our priests have the unique role to speak truth and call all of us back to the love of Christ through the sacraments and by sharing the Gospel message. To counter this great epidemic of hardheartedness that prevents us from being moved to pity or respond with tender feelings, we need to throw ourselves into God's ocean of mercy to jumpstart our hearts with grace and love. For this reason, two of the most important virtues the Sacred Heart of Jesus desires to grow in us are charity and humility.

St. Margaret Mary said, "Let us refrain carefully from saying anything, especially on occasions where we are humiliated. Let us be charitable and humble in thoughts and word. I firmly believe that if you find yourself faithful in all this, the adorable Heart of Jesus will be more liberal with his graces to you than He ever has been before, and will love you tenderly."[5]

Preaching that penetrates hearts all comes from Jesus. A priest once shared that he knows the Lord is with him when he preaches because he gets a wide range of meaningful spiritual feedback after Mass. Each listener hears what they need to hear, and oftentimes the message received is very different. I have found this to be so true. I have left Mass hearing what I needed to hear, and yet my husband received a different message from the same readings or homily.

Charity and humility are both essential for priests who want to deliver homilies and preach in a way that will reach the listener without unduly offending. The same is true for the laity, as we cannot promote this message of God's love without making room for humble charity in our own hearts. The Sacred Heart reminds us of the love God has for us, and that love needs to go forth to others. We can't just place the image or statue of the Sacred Heart up in our home or Church and expect the holy image to impact hearts. No, the image is a constant reminder that we have been called to share the warmth of God.

Once we have opened our hearts and homes to the truth of God and the love he has for us, we will be inspired to go forth and live worthy lives. Once we have been set free and washed clean of sin, we will want to remain in that state of grace, and not fall into the same traps that once held us captive. We will seek opportunities to receive the sacraments and share the love of Jesus with others who are still struggling to overcome sin and be healed of their wounds.

Is it any wonder, then, that most fervent ambassadors for Christ were once the greatest of sinners? Released from the pain that comes from a sinful lifestyle, they are set free—and want nothing more than to share that freedom with others.

PONDERING THE PROMISE

The Church and the sacraments are gifts for transforming our lives and unleashing new graces. When we seek out the sacrament of confession, we come to know that our sins are forgiven and receive the graces we need to live out our Christian faith. Jesus is exposing to us his all-merciful and loving heart—he wants to soften our hearts and make them more like his. Jesus wants our sacrifices done in love to show him that we love him in return. Let's think about that for a moment.

1. Do you know that the Lord wants to have a personal relationship with you and forgive you of your sins? He died for you so you can be with him forever in heaven. Is it hard for you to say, "I am sorry"?
2. Do you believe the Lord gave us the ordained priesthood to administer graces here on earth? Do you see Christ in the priest when you go to confession? Can you see your own heart being transformed in the sacrament? If you have not been to confession in a long time, what holds you back from this sacrament? (Reread CCC, 1423–24.)
3. "If we acknowledge our sins, he is faithful and just and will forgive us" (1 Jn 1:9). How do you see this reading playing out in your life? Do you find it freeing to release your sins through confession?
4. "This people honors me with their lips, but their heart are far from me" (Mt 15:8). How can we go the next step and honor the Lord not just with our lips but by surrendering our whole hearts for healing and softening?

PRAYING THE PROMISE

In a world where many seek to dethrone the Lord in their lives, as members of the body of Christ we have an opportunity to help atone for the failings of others and to intercede on their behalf. This prayer is a powerful reminder of how our sins impact Jesus, yet he is always there to comfort us, forgive us, and invite us to love him more completely.

PRAYER OF REPARATION TO THE SACRED HEART OF JESUS

Adorable Heart of Jesus, glowing with love for us and inflamed with zeal for our salvation. O Heart that understands the misery to which our sins have brought us, infinitely rich in mercy to heal the wounds of our souls, behold me humbly kneeling before You to express the sorrow that fills my heart for the coldness and indifference with which I have so long returned the numberless benefits which You have bestowed upon me.

With a deep sense of the outrages that have been heaped upon You by my sins and the sins of others, I wish to make reparation to Your most Sacred Majesty. It was our sins that filled Your Heart with bitterness; it was the weight of our guilt that pressed down Your face to the earth in the Garden of Olives and caused you to die in agony on the Cross. But now, repentant and sorrowful, I implore Your forgiveness.

Adorable Heart of Jesus, Source of true consolation and ever merciful to the penitent sinner, impart to our hearts the spirit of penance that we may be sincerely sorry for our sins. Pardon them, O Lord, in Your mercy, and let all who have sinned against You in the Sacrament of Your love be converted and return to You. Deliver us from our sins. And in order to repair the sins of ingratitude by which we have grieved Your most tender and loving Heart, may we love and honor You in the most adorable Sacrament of the Altar, where You are present to hear and grant our petitions and to be the food and life of our souls.

Merciful Jesus, be our Mediator with Your heavenly Father, whom we have so grievously offended. Help us to amend our ways. As Your Sacred Heart is our refuge and our hope when we have sinned, so let it be the strength and support of our repentance, and nothing in life or death shall ever separate us from You.

Amen.[6]

PRACTICING THE PROMISE

How often do you go to confession? This is a great first step for those who want to soften their hearts in order to let Jesus enter and reign there. Going to confession regularly—even every couple of months—will help you to move toward a closer relationship with Jesus' Sacred Heart, as the graces of the sacrament anoint and transform every aspect of your life. You can read more about this sacrament in the *Catechism* (1423–24).

Make plans to go to reconciliation this week with your family. Offer the Litany of the Sacred Heart of Jesus as a sign of your sincerity to fulfill this intention.

11

Share the Sacred Heart Devotion with Others

Promise #11

Those who shall promote this devotion shall have their names written in my heart.

> Happy are those whom the Sacred Heart of Jesus will employ in establishing his reign. . . . When this Heart reigns victorious on its thorn, it will be itself their eternal recompense.
>
> —St. Margaret Mary[1]

It is one thing to choose to grow in holiness and practice our Catholic faith, living a life committed to the most Sacred Heart; it is another to become an evangelist and live a life of sharing this devotion with others. My parents instilled the need to evangelize in a way that inspired all four of us children to remain strong in our conviction that Christ is the solution to all our trials and troubles.

I witnessed firsthand the impact this devotion can have on someone's life by watching my parents' and grandparents' faith deepen through this powerful and stable devotion. They came to appreciate what it means to love Christ and share that love with others through promoting this devotion. This promise is about not only becoming holy but also being willing to share your faith and devotion to the Sacred Heart with others.

In 1988, my family took a bold step of faith by enthroning the Sacred Heart of Jesus as king, savior, and friend in our home. He was officially welcomed into our home, no longer knocking outside on the doors of our hearts. The person who led us through the enthronement was Fr. Joe, our family priest friend, a very soft-spoken and humble man who boldly depended on the Lord for guidance. The day we did the enthronement he was there to bless our home and witness the enthronement to the Sacred Heart of Jesus.

There were no firecrackers on that enthronement day. As teenagers, we still fought over how the other people in our family were praying, picked on each other for how quickly the prayers were said . . . and yet we also received special graces. On that day, when the Sacred Heart image was put in our home in a place of honor, we went from being a culturally Catholic family to one that was starting to take steps toward deepening in faith. We started to live out our Catholic faith by not just going to Mass on Sunday morning but also praying as a family, living out the liturgical seasons, and talking about our faith around the dinner table. My mom and dad started to point out the "miracles" in our lives, and slowly the culture of our family changed. We liked this new way of relating, and we saw that our Catholic faith wasn't boring.

Some thirty years later, a local ministry started by my parents, Sacred Heart Columbus, has more than eighty missionaries that witness enthronements to the Sacred Heart, which led to our launching an initiative to promote the devotion nationally. We began with a monthly radio program on our local Catholic radio station and an annual Sacred Heart Congress, which provides a day of prayer and formation centered on the devotion. In our city alone, more than 2,500 homes have been enthroned over the last ten years. All of this was through the grace of God! Only Jesus can solve our problems, heal, comfort, console, strengthen, and help those whose names have been written in his heart.

EXPLORING THE PROMISE

> I wish to express my approval and encouragement to all who in any way continue to foster, study and promote devotion to the Heart of Christ in the Church with language and forms adapted to our times, so that it may be transmitted to future generations in the spirit which has always animated it.
>
> —St. John Paul II[2]

This is one of the most meaningful and powerful statements in modern history regarding a great devotion like the Sacred Heart. This quote is pointing to the need to share this devotion with others and reach out to our peers in the best way possible. Like any powerful devotion or expression of faith, we need to evaluate how to proclaim the Gospel message in a way that is perceived as both relevant and life-changing. Jesus spent three years teaching and forming his disciples; as Catholic Christians we too need to learn how to promote the faith and to share it with others.

All our actions of evangelization must first come forth from prayers. St. Margaret Mary writes,

> The adorable Heart of Jesus wishes to establish the reign of his pure love in all hearts. Happy are those whom He will employ to aid him to establish his reign! But He did not tell me that his friends would have nothing to suffer, for He wishes them to make their greatest happiness consist in tasting its bitterness. Let us not therefore be afraid of the pain and suffering that we shall meet with in this holy work, but rather let us esteem ourselves happy that He deems us worthy to suffer for so estimable a cause; I say, even all kinds of pains, contradictions, calumnies, and sorrow for the more of them I meet the more I am encouraged and the greatest my confidence that all my work will succeed to the glory of this loving Heart and the salvation of many souls.[3]

What a perfect reminder to "keep the faith" and persevere in our work promoting the kingdom even when it is challenging. Even more powerful is to think that Jesus set up a kingdom where all are welcomed, where the lost and forgotten are continually sought and saved.

PONDERING THE PROMISE

This promise is about God's desire to reward those who heed the great call to action. "Nor do they light a lamp and then put it under a bushel basket; it is set on a lampstand, where it gives light to all in the house. Just so, your light must shine before others, that they may see your good deeds and glorify your heavenly Father" (Mt 5:15–16).

If we are faithful, when our time on this earth is done, we will hear, "Well done, my good and faithful servant. Since you were faithful in small matters, I will give you great responsibilities. Come, share your master's joy" (Mt 25:23). Take a few moments now to consider how you can be more faithful to the opportunities to exercise your faith through this devotion to the heart of Jesus.

1. "Those who shall promote this devotion shall have their names written in my heart." Do you believe that the Lord Jesus wants to use you to share this message? How do you feel about this invitation?
2. How do you feel called to promote this teaching, in your deeds, words, or prayer?
3. If your faith were a flashlight, how far would it shine? "Nor do they light a lamp and then put it under a bushel basket; it is set on a lampstand, where it gives light to all in the house. Just so, your light must shine before others, that they may see your good deeds and glorify your heavenly Father" (Mt 5:15–16). How can this scripture manifest in

your life? How can this Gospel message come alive through promoting the devotion?

PRAYING THE PROMISE

One of the greatest gifts we can give to others is to offer up prayers on their behalf. When a loved one, friend, coworker, or even a stranger passes away, we can offer up our prayers, works, and deeds for their eternal salvation. When we pray for all of mankind, we grow in empathy for others and the perfection of our own soul increases.

PRAYER FOR ALL MANKIND

O Divine Heart of Jesus, grant I pray Thee, eternal rest to the souls in purgatory,
the final grace to those who are about to die, true repentance to sinners,
the light of faith to unbelievers, and Your grace to me and to all who are dear to me.
To you, therefore, O Most Merciful Heart of Jesus, I commend all these souls,
and in their behalf I offer You all Your merits in union with the merits of Your most blessed Mother and of all the angels and saints, together with all the Masses,
Communions, prayers and good works which are this day being offered throughout the world.
Amen.[4]

PRACTICING THE PROMISE

How can the Lord employ you to pass on the kingdom of love? Could you share the image of the Sacred Heart with others? What small deeds could you do this week to promote the devotion? Perhaps you could write a letter or send an e-mail to friends sharing what you have learned or what this devotion means to you and encourage them to welcome the Sacred Heart into their lives.

This devotion is also about teaching others to pray. Oftentimes families do not know how to pray the Holy Rosary when they begin the enthronement. This prayer leads you to Jesus, for it focuses on the life of Christ. I recommend starting with one decade of the Rosary, for most families no longer know how to pray this prayer, but my hope is that you learn to pray this whole prayer and share this devotion with your family. To learn more, visit welcomehisheart.com/how-to-pray-the-rosary.

In closing, offer the Litany of the Sacred Heart of Jesus.

12

TURN TO THE EUCHARIST FOR STRENGTH AND SPIRITUAL FOOD

Promise #12

My divine Heart shall be their safe refuge in the last moments.

I promise you in the excessive mercy of my Heart that my all-powerful love will grant to all those who receive Holy Communion on the First Fridays in nine consecutive months the grace of final perseverance; they shall not die in my disgrace, nor without receiving their sacraments. My divine Heart shall be their safe refuge in this last moment.

—Jesus to St. Margaret Mary[1]

This promise, known as the "Great Promise," is one of the greatest gifts you can receive. The twelve promises are not magical, nor should we use them to keep score with God. Rather, these promises present opportunities for us to seek out graces emanating from the heart of the Savior, so that our lives can be transformed.

The same is true of the First Friday observation—there is nothing magical or superstitious about it. Rather, participating in this aspect of the Sacred Heart devotion is a natural expression of a heart that is already attuned to God. Jesus wants to keep this love relationship going, day after day, month after month, not just after a consecration or enthronement, but throughout our lives until the moment we rest our heads on his heart in heaven.

I have not always been successful in fulfilling my First Friday devotion: a kid will get sick, I will forget to go to Mass, or it just won't work with my schedule. However, no matter what, I try to remember that God knows my intention to fulfill this commitment and to keep on trying to live out my faith and pass it on to my family. Similarly, if you find you are unable to observe this holy habit every month, don't get discouraged or give up. Instead, choose to answer the call to holiness each day.

Each First Friday is a new beginning and opportunity to set some time aside to pray, reflect, worship our Lord, and yes, go to Mass. Each First Friday should be a special time to ponder this promise, to ask the Lord to fulfill it in your life and pray for the time to live this devotion out wholeheartedly.

Perhaps the most moving thing about this last promise is when I see the joyful anticipation of seeing the Lord in those who die while practicing this special devotion. I think of my grandfather, who prayed, worked and served, and trusted in this promise that Jesus would grant him a peaceful death with the sacraments at the end of his life.

The day he was going to die, he was in the hospital suffering from congestive heart failure and was on an oxygen mask to help him breathe. He wasn't anxious; rather, his spirits were joyful, and he was even trying to tell jokes as he always did. He spoke about how excited he was to see his parents and those who had gone before him. My mom told the nurse we needed a priest, and she said, "I can get you a chaplain if you would like; the priest isn't able to come today." It was the priest's day off, and there was bad weather. Just then, another local priest arrived on the floor in a golf shirt to visit his relative. Fortunately, a nurse recognized him and directed him to my grandfather, who died shortly after receiving confession and last rites.

My elderly grandpa had complete trust and confidence that the Sacred Heart was with him and would strengthen him. He believed that this promise from Jesus would be fulfilled because he had already experienced so many blessings from a lifetime of service to Jesus and the Church that he attributed to the Sacred Heart. When we live a life devoted to the Sacred Heart,we also are always ready for our Lord, and he never abandons us.

EXPLORING THE PROMISE

The story above is just one of many stories of those who were able to receive the sacraments before they died. "I promise you in the excessive mercy of my Heart that my all-powerful love will grant to all those who receive

Holy Communion on the First Fridays in nine consecutive months the grace of final perseverance; they shall not die in my disgrace, nor without receiving their sacraments. My divine Heart shall be their safe refuge in this last moment," said Jesus to St. Margaret Mary.

This unique promise holds specific expectations of us, and yet it is more an invitation to invest in a lifestyle of attending Mass more frequently and to renew this commitment each month. Going to Mass on the first Friday of each month helps us to reflect upon the death of our Lord: Since Jesus died on Friday, we give Jesus the first Friday of each month in reparation and to seek our spiritual food from above.

The Eucharist is our daily food, our ticket to eternal life. "Whoever eats this bread will live forever" (Jn 6:58). "The Eucharist is the source and summit of the Christian life" (*CCC*, 1324). As Catholics, we believe that it *is* the Body of Christ. If this is true, then it can be said that the Holy Eucharist and the Sacred Heart of Jesus are one and the same. Oftentimes this devotion has been called "the Devotion" since the Sacred Heart focuses on the essence of the person of Jesus. "Contemplation of the Heart of Jesus in the Eucharist will spur the faithful to seek in that Heart the inexhaustible mystery of the priesthood of Christ and of the Church. It will enable them to taste, in communion with their brothers and sisters, the spiritual sweetness of charity at its very source."[2]

The most important element of this promise is to live your faith out daily. What better way is there to do this than to grow closer to Jesus by going to Mass and receiving the Holy Eucharist? St. Claude de la Colombiere, St. Margaret Mary's spiritual director, shared, "God is more honored by a single Mass than He could be by all actions of angels and men together, however fervent and heroic they might be. . . . If we only knew the treasure we hold in our hands. . . . In the adorable Sacrifice they can find all things: graces, richness, spiritual and temporal, favors, for the body and mind for life and eternity."[3]

When we trust in the Lord and humbly live out our Catholic faith, we can accept the graces Jesus is offering us through going to Mass and living out a vibrant faith life. Many Catholics have slipped away from going to Mass on holy days of obligation and Sundays, and yet the Lord is offering us strength and graces. Jesus wants to be intimately connected with us. This promise is an invitation to not only practice the First Friday devotion but also live out your Catholic faith in the best way possible to draw closer to our Lord.

The First Friday devotion is an invitation to recall the greatest sacrifice: Jesus' death on the Cross at Calvary. When we go to Mass on First Friday, we pause in our busy life and renew our love for Christ, and in return, we allow him to express that love for us. This love is not merely a feeling but an action expressed in the most powerful way possible: Jesus dying on a Cross and giving us his body, blood, soul, and divinity in the Holy Eucharist, where we can be fed spiritually through learning to trust and receive the love and mercy of Jesus.

The particular purpose of the First Friday devotions is to offer reparation for the countless offenses committed against the Sacred Heart of Jesus.

> Behold this Heart which has loved men so much that it has spared itself nothing, even to exhausting and consuming itself, in order to testify its love. In return, I receive from the greatest part only ingratitude, by their irreverence and sacrilege, and by the coldness and contempt they have for me. . . . [Therefore, set aside] the Octave of the Feast of Corpus Christi . . . honoring my heart.[4]

The requirements for fulfilling the devotion and obtaining the promise are to receive Holy Communion on the first Friday of nine consecutive months, as our Lord instructed, and to intend to make reparation to the Sacred Heart. Reparation is when we are willing to make amends for the wrong others have done, or to act in a way of repairing something. In these days of great turmoil in society and the Catholic Church, there is a great need to begin or renew our devotion to the Sacred Heart of Jesus and embrace this devotion with a new resolution to love Christ and make up for the sins of others.

The First Friday devotion means taking time out of our busy lives to remember Jesus' atoning death as the perfect Lamb of God. As Catholics, we believe that we can cooperate with these redemptive graces by responding to Jesus' invitation and seeking to make reparations on behalf of others. We are there seeking to console the Lord for the wound of his heart—not to place blame on those who hurt Jesus (including ourselves) but rather to show him our love and desire to seek to offer reparation for this pain.

One of the great requests of Jesus to St. Margaret Mary was the celebration of the Universal Feast of the Sacred Heart. This is a great day of celebration for the gift of love Jesus is offering us, and a way to express our love for Jesus and offer up reparation for all those who do not believe, do not love, and do not adore him. May we always choose to honor and celebrate this glorious day! St. John Paul II shares that "we must have recourse to him who is the Way, the Truth and the Life. We have gone astray and we must return to the right path; darkness has overshadowed our minds and the gloom must be dispelled by the light of truth; death has seized upon us, and we must lay hold of life."[5]

Each year the Feast of the Sacred Heart is celebrated forty days after the Feast of Corpus Christi. This feast day, which was first shared with St. Margaret Mary as a desire that the Lord had, is not a universal feast. "The consecration of the human race in 1899 represents an extraordinary important step on the Church's journey and it is still good to renew it every year on the Feast of the Sacred Heart."[6]

PONDERING THE PROMISE

Throughout the course of this book, you have been receiving a continual invitation to draw close to the Sacred Heart of Jesus and to consider what Jesus is asking of you. His heart is so full of love and patient endurance. Even if and when you are unable to receive

Jesus sacramentally in the Eucharist, he invites you into intimate communion with him through this personal encounter with his Sacred Heart. Now consider:

1. Are you willing to surrender your life to the Sacred Heart to receive this powerful blessing? Have you seen this lived out in the life of others?
2. "Whoever eats this bread will live forever" (Jn 6:58). Do you view the Eucharist as your spiritual food? Do you have a desire to grow close to Christ in the Eucharist? Have you ever thought about enriching or deepening your spiritual life by attending daily Mass, or finding other ways to go beyond the basic requirements of being a practicing Catholic?
3. Do you seek out the face of Christ in your life? Do you trust him to provide what you need physically, spiritually, and in every other way? For we know that "my God will fully supply whatever you need, in accord with his glorious riches in Christ Jesus" (Phil 4:19).

PRAYING THE PROMISE

In keeping with the eucharistic theme of this chapter, let us offer this traditional act of spiritual communion for ourselves and for those who for whatever reason are unable to receive the graces of the Eucharist at this moment, that God would meet them at their deepest point of need.

ACT OF SPIRITUAL COMMUNION

My Jesus, I believe that you are present in the Most Holy Sacrament.

I love you above all things, and I desire to receive you into my soul.

Since I cannot at this moment receive you sacramentally,

Come now spiritually into my heart.

I embrace you as if you were already there,

And unite myself wholly to you.

Never permit me to be separated from you.

Amen.

PRACTICING THE PROMISE

We are invited to go to Mass on nine consecutive First Fridays and receive the Eucharist out of love for God and a spirit of reparation to the Sacred Heart of Jesus. The First Friday is a special day as it is the day the Lord died on the Cross.

If you are seeking graces for your daily journey, you need to turn to the Eucharist as your spiritual food, nourishing and strengthening your soul. The true spirit of enthronement links the image of the Sacred Heart at home with the altar at the church. You cannot develop a relationship with the Sacred Heart without understanding this powerful connection with the Eucharist. Enthronement to the Sacred Heart doesn't replace going to Mass and receiving Holy Communion, but it makes a connection that is meant to inspire you to live out your faith at home. Try to attend Mass more often to discover the heart of Jesus is the same Jesus of the Holy Eucharist.

One more time, please offer the Litany of the Sacred Heart of Jesus.

ACKNOWLEDGMENTS

I would like to start out by thanking the whole team at Ave Maria Press for allowing me to publish this book with you. Thank you for allowing me to work directly with Heidi Saxton; not only is she talented, but I consider her a friend in Christ who has gently nudged me over the last few years to bring this book to reality. Thank you, Tom Grady, and your entire team. It is a pleasure working with each of you!

I would also like to thank to my immediate family, including my siblings and extended family and friends for their love and inspiration to "do all things for Christ." Thanks especially to my parents, who introduced me to the Sacred Heart devotion; your faith is so inspiring. I love doing ministry work with you, especially on the radio.

Thank you, Sacred Heart Enthronement Network, its board of directors, and Sacred Heart Enthronement Missionaries, for your support of this book project and for desiring to bring the Sacred Heart Devotion to Catholics! I would especially like to thank Fr. Stash Dailey for serving as our spiritual director; your priesthood is a gift to so many!

I would like to thank Kimberly Hahn for her strong endorsement. It is an honor to receive such praise from a woman who has inspired me for years to grow closer to Christ. I would also like to thank Megan Schieber, coauthor of *The Theology of Home;* you are a friend in

Christ who has taught me so much and inspired me to love His Heart more each day. I am so grateful to all those who took time to read and endorse the book: Danielle Bean, Professor Gregory Haake, and Fr. David Reid, S.S.C.C. (the Congregation of the Sacred Hearts of Jesus and Mary). Thank you to everyone else that has said yes to spreading the heart of Jesus. I notice your kindness and hold it close to my heart.

Finally, I would like to acknowledge the authors and publishers whose works have been reproduced in this book:

"Sacred Heart of Jesus." Copyrighted Classic Image by Adolfo Simeone, Cromo NB Italy, www.cromo.com.

Permission to use excerpts from *Enthronement to the Sacred Heart,* copyright 1999 by Fr. Francis Larkin and from *Jesus King of Love,* copyright 1997 by Fr. Mateo Crawley-Boevey is granted from the National Enthronement Center in Fairhaven, Massachusetts.

Excerpts from *Thoughts and Sayings of St. Margaret Mary: For Every Day of the Year* (1986 edition) and from "The Letters from St. Margaret Mary to Father Croiset, S.J.," in *The Devotion to the Sacred Heart of Jesus Christ: How to Practice the Sacred Heart Devotion,* by Jean Croiset et al. (1988 edition) are published by Tan Books in Rockford, Illinois.

APPENDIX 1

A BRIEF HISTORY OF THE SACRED HEART IN THE CHURCH

The devotion to the Sacred Heart of Jesus has been cherished by many throughout the history of the Church and has enriched Catholic spirituality for centuries. Clergy, religious, and even professed saints have affirmed this powerful devotion and revealed that Jesus' Most Sacred Heart is a fount of goodness, love, and mercy and a path to authentic holiness.

THE MESSENGERS

In the pages that follow, we will focus on some of the most important of these witnesses to this powerful devotion: St. Gertrude (thirteenth-century mystic and Doctor of the Church), St. Margaret Mary Alacoque (seventeenth-century French Visitation nun), and Fr. Mateo Crawley-Boevey (twentieth-century Peruvian Father of Enthronement of the Sacred Heart).

St. Gertrude

THE HERALD OF DIVINE LOVE

> I wish your writings to be for later times a proof of the tenderness of My Heart, and I will make them a source of grace to many souls.
>
> —From Jesus to St. Gertrude[1]

A thirteenth-century mystic and Doctor of the Church known as the "Herald of Divine Love," St. Gertrude had a great desire to make the Sacred Heart devotion known and loved. In 1281, twenty-five-year-old Gertrude experienced her first series of visions that would continue until the end of her life (and have since been approved by the Catholic Church). These visions reordered her priorities and led her to share with great fervor the message of Jesus' love to all of humanity.

In her writings, St. Gertrude revealed that she once had a vision in which she spoke with the apostle John about the moment at the Last Supper when he rested his head on Jesus' chest: "One of his disciples, the one whom Jesus loved, was reclining at Jesus' side" (Jn 13:23). In the most stressful moment in the life of Christ, when one of his closest followers was about to betray him, St. John sought out his holy heart and rested in that place of comfort and security. This is where the beloved disciple took his refuge, showing us where we too should turn when life is difficult.

Later the following day, from the foot of the Cross, St. John witnessed the piercing of that same heart. "But one soldier thrust his lance into his side, and immediately blood and water flowed out" (Jn 19:34). Again, the scriptures speak to the reality of the piercing of Jesus' heart. His heart, broken open for all of us, is a gift offered by Christ to us, one that he longs for us to accept. So great is his longing for us to understand that Jesus continues to show us the way through yet another ambassador later in history.

In that vision, St. Gertrude asked St. John why he did not share his experience of hearing the heartbeat of Christ in his gospel writings. St. John answered, "My ministry in those early times of the Church was confined to speaking of the Divine Word, the eternal son of the Father, some words of deep meaning upon which human intelligence might meditate forever . . . but for these latter times was reserved the grace of hearing the eloquent voice of the Heart of Jesus. At this voice the time-worn world will renew its youth, be roused from its lethargy, and again be inflamed with the warm Divine love."[2]

These powerful words strike at our hearts when we feel burned out and in need of revival not only in our churches and parishes but also in our hearts and homes. We can all relate to living in a society that has grown weary and exhausted and needs to be inflamed with the warmth of divine love. Only divine love will transform hearts and set them on fire. Only divine love will transform the face of the earth and set it ablaze with faith. Through his actions, St. John points us toward his heart and demonstrates how important the heart of Jesus is in the life of the Church. This beautiful devotion focuses on the very person of Jesus. It is Christ-focused and leads us to better know and love our Lord.

St. Margaret Mary

THE APOSTLE OF THE SACRED HEART

> Devotion to the Sacred Heart is a last effort of the Savior to draw sinners to repentance and to give

them abundantly efficacious and sanctifying graces to work out their salvation.

—From Jesus to St. Margaret Mary[3]

St. Margaret Mary Alacoque received visions from Jesus in the latter part of the seventeenth century. Jesus appeared to her to show her his burning heart and shared how much he loved her and the whole world and desired to develop a deeper relationship with humanity.

This great saint was born in the diocese of Autun (France) on July 22, 1647, the fifth of seven children. Even as a child, she had a deep love for the Lord and always wanted to please him. She was also deeply devoted to Our Lady. While growing up, St. Margaret Mary only had two years of formal learning from the Urbanist nuns, yet her contributions to the Church have been significant. At the age of nine, she experienced true intimacy with Jesus by receiving her first Holy Communion. She would write, "This Communion shed such bitterness over all my little pleasures and amusements that I was no longer able to enjoy any of them, although I sought them eagerly."[4]

After this she became extremely ill and was even unable to walk for about four years, as she recorded in her letters. "But I fell into so pitiable a state of ill health that for about four years I was unable to walk. My bones pierced my skin . . . since no remedy could be found for my illness, I was consecrated to the Blessed Virgin with the promise that, if she cured me, I should one day be one of her daughters."[5] St. Margaret Mary was cured, and in 1671, she joined the Visitation order at Paray-le-Monial; she professed the following year.

St. Margaret Mary experienced apparitions from Christ who revealed his most Sacred Heart to her and his deep love for mankind. All the apparitions took place while St. Margaret Mary was praying before the Blessed Sacrament or after receiving Holy Communion. She saw Christ's heart engulfed in flames and surrounded by thorns and heard his loving voice share these words: "Behold this Heart, which has loved men so much, that it has spared nothing even to exhausting and consuming Itself in order to testify to them Its love; and in return I receive from the greater number nothing but ingratitude by reason of their irreverence and sacrileges, and by the coldness and contempt they show me in the Sacrament of Love."[6] St. Margaret Mary knew Christ had selected her and, with the help of St. Claude de la Colombiere, S.J., was instrumental in instituting the great Feast of the Sacred Heart and spreading the devotion to the Sacred Heart throughout the world.

St. Margaret Mary is a saintly role model on how to love as Christ taught her. She once wrote, "True it is that one who loves does not think, even in the midst of the greatest sufferings, that he is suffering anything. But you will surely grant me that no one can love without suffering. The love of my God is a pitiless tyrant who never says 'enough.'"[7] Christ desires that we learn to love others by first loving him. The Sacred Heart of Jesus devotion is one where we allow Christ to renew us and transform our heart.

St. Margaret Mary Alacoque revealed to us not only a devotion that the world desperately needs but also a road map to holiness through loving the heart of Christ. This saint shared the messages of Christ in a way that touched even the hardest of sinners and provided so many with hope that miracles can happen when hearts unite with Christ. This wonderful saint died on October 17, 1690, at the age of forty-two and was canonized on May 13, 1920, by Pope Benedict XV.

As to the laity living in the world, they shall find in this devotion all the aids necessary in their state in life, a saving refuge during life, especially at the hour of death. It was through the witness of St. Margaret Mary that the official devotion to the Sacred Heart began, yet it was through the work of still others that it spread across the globe.

Fr. Mateo Crawley

FATHER OF ENTHRONEMENT TO THE SACRED HEART

Every generation since the birth of Christ has had heroic and holy leaders, future saints, and dreamers for God who had a clear understanding of renewal not only for their own heart but also for all people. One such individual was a simple priest who would later be called the Father of Enthronement to the Sacred Heart, Fr. Mateo Crawley-Boevey.

This priest is credited with reintroducing the Sacred Heart devotion on a worldwide scale, especially to the laity and religious alike. He knew that without this devotion, not only would souls be lost but also families would drift apart due to secularism and modernism. He would later become one of the most influential people in promoting this devotion in modern times, helping families turn to the Sacred Heart as their refuge and source of new graces.

Fr. Mateo was born on November 18, 1875, in Peru. Fr. Mateo's mission to share enthronement began after he had a miraculous healing while praying in the Chapel of Paray-le-Monial at the Visitation chapel in France, the same chapel in which St. Margaret Mary received her visions from Jesus. After his healing, he also had a clear understanding that enthronement would help all Catholics. After Fr. Mateo revealed his plan to promote enthronement to the Sacred Heart to Pope Pius X in June 1907, the pope stated, "No, my son. I command you, do you understand? Not only do I permit you, but I order you to give your life for this work of salvation. It is a wonderful work; consecrate your entire life to it."[8]

In 1915, Fr. Mateo was granted an audience with Pope Benedict XV, who later wrote a letter approving the definition of enthronement as "the installation of the image of the Sacred Heart, as on a throne, in the place of highest honor in the house, so that Jesus Christ our Lord visibly reigns in Catholic homes." The pope would also share, "Nothing is more suitable to the needs of the present day than your enterprise."[9] Enthronement is not just a passing celebration but rather a lifestyle of welcoming Jesus into the home as king, brother, savior, and friend each and every day.

Fr. Mateo shared the importance of enthronement to kings, religious, priests, lay people, and even peasants. This priest went out of his way, preaching and proclaiming this powerful devotion around the world. While touring the vast destruction of World War I throughout France, Fr. Mateo exhorted us, "Never forget that the ruin of Christian families is a greater evil still. The family is the temple of temples. The family is the source of life. . . . If Jesus Christ is inoculated in its roots, the entire tree will be Jesus Christ."[10] Fr. Mateo had a clear understanding that Catholic families were at risk and that we needed to cherish the base building block of society and its members.

PAPAL SUPPORT

In May of 1899 the world was consecrated to the Sacred Heart by Pope Leo XIII in his letter *Annum Sacrum* (May 25, 1899), partly through the inspiration of Blessed Mary of the Divine Heart, whose pious prayers and pleading convinced Leo XIII that this consecration was the will of God. Since this great event in the life of the Church, there has been papal support and even affirmation on each landmark anniversary.

On the fiftieth anniversary of this consecration, St. Pius XII released *Aquas Haurietis* (*On the Devotion to the Sacred Heart*) on May 15, 1956, which is full of spiritual insights and again a great calling for us the faithful to dedicate our lives to the Sacred Heart. On June 11, 1999, St. John Paul II wrote a letter "On the 100th Anniversary of the Consecration of the Human Race to the Divine Heart of Jesus." In this letter, he said, "Since in the Sacred Heart the believer encounters the symbol and the living image of the infinite love of Christ, which in itself spurs us to love one another, he cannot fail to recognize the need to participate personally in the work of salvation."[11] John Paul II also gives a great commission to go forth and spread this devotion in the times we live in: "I wish to express my approval and encouragement to all who in any way continue to foster, study and promote devotion to the Heart of Christ in the Church with language and forms adapted to our times, so that it may be transmitted to future generations in the spirit which has always animated it."[12] These words are calling forth a great commission to rediscover the heartbeat of God in a manner that is relatable to the modern world. Besides official letters, many popes have referred to this devotion as a source of great importance in the spiritual life, assuring us that this devotion is nestled in the heart of the Church, leading us to Jesus.

APPENDIX 2

THE LITANY OF THE SACRED HEART

On Good Friday of 2020, Archbishop José H. Gomez of Los Angeles reminded the faithful of the power of the Litany of the Sacred Heart as he prayed to God to bring about an end to COVID-19. In his homily the archbishop said, "As we stand today at the foot of his cross, in the midst of this pandemic, Jesus is calling us to trust in His Sacred Heart. Let's pray often to the Sacred Heart of Jesus: 'Jesus, I trust in you!'"[1]

This significant moment brings to light our need to return to Christ during difficult trials, and serves as a powerful reminder that the Litany of the Sacred Heart is a prayer for all times. This prayer has been not only the comfort of many Catholics over the years but a powerful way to grow in your love for Jesus' holy heart.[2]

Over time the form of this litany has evolved, according to the needs of the faithful. It was first approved for public use in 1899, by Pope Leo XIII; however, the roots of this prayer can be traced back another two hundred years, to Fr. John Croiset, the spiritual director of St. Margaret Mary (1647–1690). At that time, the litany contained just seventeen lines; an additional thirty-three lines (the petitions invoking the "Heart of Jesus") were later added to represent the thirty-three years of the life of Christ.

The Catholic Church holds such value in praying this litany that it has sanctioned a *partial indulgence for its recitation.*[3] Praying the Litany of the Sacred Heart each time you finish a chapter of this book will help you grow closer to the Heart of Jesus and focus on the thirty-three years of his earthly life. As we focus on the life of Jesus, we come to recognize the gift of our earthly life! This litany helps us to worship and honor Jesus, and to ask Him for help and guidance in our daily trials. (Editor's note: When the litany is prayed in a group setting, as an antiphonal reading, the leader reads the "V" [versicle] and the group reads the "R" [response].)

LITANY OF THE SACRED HEART OF JESUS

V: Lord, have mercy.
R: Lord, have mercy.
V: Christ, have mercy.
R: Christ, have mercy.
V: Lord, have mercy.
R: Lord, have mercy.

V: Christ, hear us.
R: Christ, hear us.

V: Christ, graciously hear us.
R: Christ, graciously hear us.

V: God the Father in heaven,
R: Have mercy on us.

V: God the Son, Redeemer of the World,
R: God the Holy Spirit, Holy Trinity, one God,

(Unison)
Heart of Jesus, Son of the Eternal Father,
Heart of Jesus, formed by the Holy Spirit in the womb of the Virgin Mary,
Heart of Jesus, substantially united to the Word of God,

Heart of Jesus, of infinite majesty,
Heart of Jesus, sacred temple of God,
Heart of Jesus, tabernacle of the Most High,

Heart of Jesus, house of God and gate of heaven,
Heart of Jesus, burning furnace of charity,
Heart of Jesus, abode of justice and love,
Heart of Jesus, full of goodness and love,
Heart of Jesus, wellspring of all virtues,
Heart of Jesus, most worthy of all praise,
Heart of Jesus, King and center of all hearts,
Heart of Jesus, in whom are all the treasures of wisdom and knowledge,

Heart of Jesus, in whom dwells the fullness of divinity,
Heart of Jesus, in whom the Father was well pleased,
Heart of Jesus, of whose fullness we have all received,
Heart of Jesus, desire of the everlasting hills,
Heart of Jesus, patient and most merciful,
Heart of Jesus, enriching all who invoke you,
Heart of Jesus, fountain of life and holiness,
Heart of Jesus, atonement for our sins,
Heart of Jesus, overwhelmed with insults,
Heart of Jesus, bruised for our offenses,
Heart of Jesus, obedient unto death,

Heart of Jesus, pierced with a lance,
Heart of Jesus, source of all consolation,
Heart of Jesus, our life and resurrection,
Heart of Jesus, our peace and reconciliation,
Heart of Jesus, victim of sins,
Heart of Jesus, salvation of those who trust in you,
Heart of Jesus, hope of those who die in you,
Heart of Jesus, delight of all saints,

Lamb of God, who takes away the sins of the world, spare us, O Lord.
Lamb of God, who takes away the sins of the world, graciously hear us, O Lord.
Lamb of God, who takes away the sins of the world, have mercy on us.

V. Jesus, meek and humble of heart.
R. Make our hearts like unto thine.

V: Let us pray.
R: Almighty and Eternal God, look upon the heart of your dearly beloved Son and upon the praise and satisfaction he offers you in the name of sinners and for those who seek your mercy; be appeased, and grant us pardon in the name of the same Jesus Christ, your Son, who lives and reigns with you forever and ever. Amen.

Notes

INTRODUCTION

1. Jean Bainvel, "Devotion to the Sacred Heart of Jesus," in *The Catholic Encyclopedia*, vol. 7 (New York: Appleton, 1910), New Advent, accessed March 3, 2020, http://www.newadvent.org.

2. Francis Larkin, *Understanding the Heart* (Orlando, FL: Reconciliation Press, 1975), 28–29.

1. ALLOW GRACE TO FILL YOUR LIFE

1. Margaret Mary Alacoque, *Thoughts and Sayings of St. Margaret Mary: For Every Day of the Year* (Rockford, IL: Tan Books, 1986), 39.

2. Francis Larkin, *Enthronement of the Sacred Heart* (Fairhaven, MA: National Enthronement Center, 1999), 59.

3. Quoted in Claudia Carlen, *The Papal Encyclicals: Leo XIII, Encyclical Annum Sacrum* (Wilmington, NC: McGrath, 1981), 75–76.

4. Margaret Mary Alacoque, *The Autobiography of St. Margaret Mary* (Rockford, IL: Tan Books, 1986), 117–18.

2. WELCOME CHRIST'S PEACE IN YOUR HOME

1. John Croiset, *The Devotion to the Sacred Heart of Jesus: How to Practice the Sacred Heart Devotion*. (Rockford, IL: Tan Books and Publisher Inc. 1988), 244.

2. Alacoque, *Thoughts and Sayings*, 34.

3. Augustine, "The Confessions (Book I)," trans. J. G. Pilkington, revised and edited by Kevin Knight, New Advent, http://www.newadvent.org. From *Nicene and Post-Nicene Fathers*, First Series, vol. 1, ed. Philip Schaff (Buffalo, NY: Christian Literature Publishing, 1887).

4. Alacoque, *Thoughts and Sayings*, 34.

5. Sacred Heart Enthronement Network, *Welcome His Heart Enthronement Booklet* (Columbus, OH: Self-Publish, 2019).

6. Margaret Mary Alacoque, *The Letters of St. Margaret Mary Alacoque*: Apostle of the Sacred Heart, *trans. Clarence A. Herbst* (Rockford, IL: Tan Books, 1997), introduction, xii.

7. "Franciscan and Other Common Prayers: Prayer of Saint Francis of Assisi," *Franciscan Sisters of Perpetual Adoration (FSPA)*, December 17, 2019, http://www.fspa.org.

3. OFFER YOUR STRUGGLES TO JESUS

1. Pius XII, *Haurietis Aquas* (May 15, 1956)

2. Quoted in Larkin, *Understanding the Heart* (Orlando, FL: Reconciliation Press, 1975,) 38.

3. Alacoque, *Thoughts and Sayings*, 78.

4. "The Letters from St. Margaret Mary to Father Croiset, S.J.," in *The Devotion to the Sacred Heart of Jesus Christ: How to Practice the Sacred Heart Devotion*, by Jean Croiset et al. (Rockford, IL: Tan Books, 1988), 255.

5. *St. Francis of Assisi and the Conversion of the Muslims,* edited by Frank M. Rega (Rockford, IL: Tan Books, 2008), 114.

6. "A Morning Offering," Our Catholic Prayers, accessed October 15, 2019, http://www.ourcatholicprayers.com.

4. TAKE REFUGE IN JESUS

1. Quoted in Francis Larkin, *Enthronement to the Sacred Heart of Jesus* (Fairhaven, MA: National Enthronement Center, 1999), 44.

2. Mateo Crawley-Boevey, *Jesus, King of Love* (Fairhaven, MA: National Enthronement Center, 1997), 230.

3. Crawley-Boevey, *Jesus, King of Love*, 230.

4. Alacoque, *Letters of St. Margaret Mary Alacoque*, 31.

5. "A Prayer for Myself," in Larkin, *Enthronement of the Sacred Heart*, 541.

5. RECOGNIZE JESUS' BLESSING AND GUIDANCE

1. Alacoque, *Thoughts and Sayings*, 65.

2. Alacoque, *Thoughts and Sayings*, 68.

6. ACCEPT JESUS' MERCY AND SHOW MERCY TO OTHERS

1. Quoted in Larkin, *Enthronement of the Sacred Heart*, 48.

2. Marian Fathers of the Immaculate Conception of the B.V.M., "The Sacred Heart and Divine Mercy," Divine Mercy, February 9, 2006, http://www.thedivinemercy.org.

3. Quoted in Larkin, *Enthronement of the Sacred Heart*, 48.

4. Quoted in Larkin, *Enthronement of the Sacred Heart*, 48.

5. Maria Faustina Kowalska, *Diary: Divine Mercy in My Soul*, 3rd ed. (Stockbridge, MA: Marian Press, 1987), 742.

6. Quoted in Larkin, *Enthronement of the Sacred Heart*, 46.

7. Croiset, *The Devotion to the Sacred Heart of Jesus*, 321.

7. PRAY TO BE SET ON FIRE WITH THE LOVE OF CHRIST

1. Alacoque, *Thoughts and Sayings*, 82.

2. Quoted in Joseph Keller, *The Sacred Heart: Anecdotes and Examples to Assist in Promoting the Devotion to the Sacred Heart* (New York: Benziger Brothers, 1899), 36.

3. Francis (@Pontifex), "There are two attitudes typical of lukewarm Christians . . ." on Twitter, December 16, 2019, 8:05 a.m. https://twitter.com/pontifex/status/1206561001648381953?lang=en.

4. Larkin, *Enthronement to the Sacred Heart of Jesus*, 8.

5. Quoted in Larkin, *Enthronement to the Sacred Heart of Jesus*, 9.

6. Quoted in Larkin, *Enthronement to the Sacred Heart of Jesus*, 288.

7. Interview with Fr. Stash Dailey, Spiritual Director of Sacred Heart Enthronement Network. September 8, 2019.

8. SEEK CHRIST'S PERFECTION BY PRAYING AND FASTING

1. Keller, *Sacred Heart*, 74.

2. Quoted in Phil Kilroy, "Sophie Barat's Integration of Inner Life and Spiritual Leadership of the Society," accessed December 27, 2019, http://madeleinesophiebarat.org.

3. Quoted in Larkin, *Enthronement of the Sacred Heart*, 14.

4. "St. Alphonsus Liguori," Divine Mercy, September 5, 2019, http://www.thedivinemercy.org.

5. "Mother Cabrini," Missionary Sisters of the Sacred Heart of Jesus, accessed December 27, 2019, http://www.mothercabrini.org.

6. "St. Therese and the Sacred Heart," Letter 122, Sisters of Reparation to the Most Sacred Heart of Jesus, accessed December 21, 2019, http://www.sistersofreparation.org.

7. Philip Kosloski, "5 Saintly Quotes about Devotion to the Sacred Heart," Aleteia, October 16, 2017, http://aleteia.org.

8. Quoted in Larkin, *Enthronement of the Sacred Heart*, 14.

9. "Augustine on the Psalms: Psalms 41–45," Christian Apologetics and Research Ministry, May 17, 2017, http://carm.org.

9. DEDICATE YOUR HOME (AND SCHOOL AND WORKPLACE) TO JESUS

1. Alacoque, *Letters of St. Margaret Mary Alacoque*, 101.

2. Quoted in Larkin, *Enthronement of the Sacred Heart*, 57.

3. Pius XI, *Quas Primas*, December 11, 1925, section 26, http://www.vatican.va.

4. Pius XI, *Quas Primas*, 19.

5. Quoted in Larkin, *Enthronement of the Sacred Heart*, 19.

6. Quoted in Larkin, *Enthronement of the Sacred Heart*, 288.

7. Mateo Crawley-Boevey, *Jesus, King of Love* (Fairhaven, MA: National Enthronement Center, 1997), 150.

10. CONFESS YOUR SINS AND ASK JESUS TO SOFTEN YOUR HEART

1. Quoted in Larkin, *Enthronement of the Sacred Heart*, 41.

2. Interview with Fr. Nathan Cromley. Eagle Eye Ministries. Voxer App. October 18, 2019.

3. Interview with Fr. Chas Canoy, Pastor of St. John the Evangelist Parish. Jackson, MI. October 20, 2019.

4. Quoted in Larkin, *Enthronement of the Sacred Heart*, 47.

5. Margaret Mary Alacoque, "The Prayer: Divine Heart of Jesus," Catholic Doors Ministry, accessed November 17, 2019, https://www.catholicdoors.com.

6. Margaret Mary Alacoque, "Prayers of Reparation to the Sacred Heart of Jesus," Our Catholic Prayers, accessed December, 13, 2019, http://www.ourcatholicprayers.com.

11. SHARE THE SACRED HEART DEVOTION WITH OTHERS

1. Quoted in Larkin, *Enthronement of the Sacred Heart*, 48.

2. John Paul II, "Letter of John Paul II on the 100th Anniversary of the Consecration of the Human Race to the Divine Heart of Jesus," June 11, 1999, section 2, http://www.vatican.va.

3. Quoted in Larkin, *Enthronement of the Sacred Heart*, 47.

4. Quoted in Larkin, *Enthronement of the Sacred Heart*, 287.

12. TURN TO THE EUCHARIST FOR STRENGTH AND SPIRITUAL FOOD

1. Quoted in Larkin, *Enthronement of the Sacred Heart*, 43.

2. John Paul II, "Letter of John Paul II on the 100th Anniversary of the Consecration of the Human Race to the Divine Heart of Jesus," June 11, 1999, http://www.vatican.va.

3. Quoted in John Croiset, *The Devotion to the Sacred Heart*, trans. Patrick O'Connell (Charlotte, NC: Tan Books, 1988), 128.

4. Quoted in Larkin, *Enthronement of the Sacred Heart*, 70.

5. Leo XIII, *Annum Sacrum*, May 25, 1899, http://www.vatican.va.

6. John Paul II, "Letter of John Paul II on the 100th Anniversary of the Consecration of the Human Race to the Divine Heart of Jesus," June 11, 1999, http://www.vatican.va.

APPENDIX 1. A BRIEF HISTORY OF THE SACRED HEART IN THE CHURCH

1. Quoted in Andre Prevot, *Love, Peace, and Joy: Devotion to the Sacred Heart of Jesus according to St. Gertrude* (Charlotte, NC: Tan Books, 2012), 4.

2. Quoted in Prevot, *Love, Peace, and Joy*, 2.

3. Margaret Mary Alacoque, *The Letters of St. Margaret Mary Alacoque: Apostle of the Sacred Heart, trans. Clarence A. Herbst* (Rockford, IL: Tan Books, 1997), 152.

4. Alacoque, *Letters of St. Margaret Mary Alacoque*, vii.

5. Alacoque, *Letters of St. Margaret Mary Alacoque*, vii.

6. Francis Larkin, *Enthronement of the Sacred Heart*. 14

7. Alacoque, *Letters of St. Margaret Mary Alacoque*, xiv.

8. Quoted in Larkin, *Enthronement of the Sacred Heart*, 54.

9. Quoted in Larkin, *Enthronement of the Sacred Heart*, 57.

10. Dom Antoine Marie O.S.B. "Dear Friend of Saint Joseph Abbey." www.clairval.com/lettres/en/2008/03/03/2050308.htm. Accessed November 15, 2020.

11. John Paul II, "Letter of John Paul II on the 100th Anniversary of the Consecration of the Human Race to the Divine Heart of Jesus," June 11, 1999, section 1, http://www.vatican.va.

12. John Paul II, "Letter of John Paul II on the 100th Anniversary of the Consecration of the Human Race to the Divine Heart of Jesus," June 11, 1999, section 2, http://www.vatican.va.

APPENDIX 2. THE LITANY OF THE SACRED HEART

1. Julie Asher, "Gomez: On Good Friday, in pandemic, Jesus asks us to trust in Sacred Heart." April 4, 2020. *Catholic News Agency*. Accessed April 20, 2020. https://www.catholicnews.com/services/english-news/2020/gomez-on-good-friday-in-pandemic-jesus-asks-us-to-trust-in-sacred-heart.cfm

2. Currently, there are only five litanies of prayer that are authorized by the Catholic Church for public prayer services. These are the Litany of the Saints, Litany of the Blessed Virgin, Litany of the Holy Name of Jesus, Litany of the Sacred Heart, and Litany of St. Joseph.

3. "Litany of the Sacred Heart," *EWTN Global Catholic Television Network*, accessed April 20, 2020, www.ewtn.com/catholicism/teachings/litany-to-the-sacred-heart-of-jesus-270.

Emily Jaminet is executive director of the Sacred Heart Enthronement Network and coauthor of *Divine Mercy for Moms, The Friendship Project, Pray Fully,* and *Our Friend Faustina*. She serves on the board of directors of the Columbus Catholic Women's Conference.

Jaminet earned a bachelor's degree in mental health and human services from Franciscan University of Steubenville in 1998. She offers a daily segment called *A Mother's Moment* on St. Gabriel Catholic Radio and Mater Dei Radio. She has spoken to several women's groups and conferences, including 1:38 Women, Mothering with Grace Annual Mother's Conference, Indiana Catholic Women's Conference, Women's Day of Reflection for Homeschoolers, and the online Catholic Conference for Moms. Jaminet has appeared on EWTN's *At Home with Jim and Joy* and a number of Catholic radio programs. She is a contributor to CatholicMom.com.

Along with her coauthor, Michele Faehnle, Jaminet received the Bishop John King Mussio Award from Franciscan University of Steubenville, of which she is an alumna. She and her husband, John, have seven children and live in Columbus, Ohio.

welcomehisheart.com
inspirethefaith.com

Facebook: Emily Jaminet - A Mother's Moment